DON'T

SAVE THE

MANNA

By

Dawn E Johnecheck

Edited by Toni Ginger (www.fiverr.com/tonnygingers)

Disclaimer

All the material contained in this book is provided for educational and informational purposes only. No responsibility can be taken for any results or outcomes resulting from the use of this material.

While every attempt has been made to provide information that is both accurate and effective, the author does not assume any responsibility for the accuracy or use/misuse of this information.

Throughout this book I have made a point of capitalizing any and all references to God. This includes, but is not limited to words like He, Him, Father, God, Jesus and Holy Spirit. This is to show that I hold God in high regard, and wish to acknowledge how important He is. Likewise, I have made it a point not to capitalize any and all reference to the devil, as I do not wish to in any way elevate him.

Different versions of the Bible maybe used throughout this book for its readability or to make a point more clearly. The versions used are at the authors discretion.

Bibles referenced may include:

KJV: King James Version

NLT: New Living Translation

ASV: American Standard Version

ESV: English Standard Version

Table of Contents

DEDICATIONS

My name is on this book, however, with that in mind credit must be given to the true author, Yahweh, Father God, Jesus and the Holy Spirit. I was just the instrument, the ink in the pen. Throughout writing this book God has guided and directed me. I have felt Him leading me step by step throughout the process. Thank you God for being so very patient with me, thank You for allowing me to be the instrument You have chosen to write this book. My prayer is that He will use this book to do great works in people's lives, to touch many in a powerful way.

Now to take a moment to thank a few very important people. First of all, there is David Hendrix. Without whom I never would have even started this book. He is a dear friend and a wonderful man of God. We were talking one day when I made a comment to him, "Stop trying to save the Manna". The reply I thought he made was, "There's a book by that name". In fact, what he said was, "You need to write that book". So, the journey began. Thank you so very much, David. You were and always will be a true friend. Know that you are dearly loved and will always be an important part of our lives.

Next, of course, is my family, my husband in particular, has been both challenging and great at pointing out things, usually from a biblical point of view. My children, God bless all three of them. They have tried and tested me in so very many ways. They challenge me and make me stretch, which helps me to grow. Of course, appreciating these things at the time doesn't always happen. Later, when there has been time to think about it, I am always amazed, at how God uses my family.

There was a wonderful dear lady in my life for only a short time, by the name of Eleanor. Eleanor was a woman that started out as a "difficult client" when I was doing home care. She quickly became not only a close friend, but also a role model. She was a woman of integrity and great faith. She had a dramatic and lasting effect on every aspect of my life. Though, we only knew each other for a few short months, before she went home to be with our father, God, I miss her very much. Someday we will sing and dance on the streets of gold together. Thank you God, for allowing me to have her in my life, even if it was only for a short while.

Many others could and should be mentioned. Those who over the years have, in one way or another had a profound effect on me and the way I see God and the world; this list however is too long. Thank you to the many whose lives have touched my own. In one way or another you have all helped me get to this point in life's great journey. My prayer is, someday we will again see each other in God's kingdom. There we will sing and dance together, with the angels, on the streets of gold.

A LITTLE ABOUT ME

So, let me tell you a little about the last few years, that have led me into writing this book.

I have always deeply believed and known that God and Jesus are real and alive. Knowing this and having a true understanding about Father God, the Holy Spirit and Jesus are two entirely different things. So many wrong ideas and misconceptions about God and the Bible floated around inside my head. Not to say it's all straightened out now. Being human, there will always be a lot of learning to do while walking God's path. Still having a tendency to go off on my own trail, God's always gracious to point me back to the right path, to guide and direct me. He is always close by, watching over us. He allows me to continue learning and growing, as He does with us all. It's a journey and it can be an exciting adventure if we let God lead the way.

As for me, I was born in the mid sixty's. Born and raised in Northern Michigan, in a small town by the name of Charlevoix. There are beaches everywhere in and around my little home town. Spent most of my time during the summer at the beach, swimming. I have also lived and traveled all over this great nation. My dad was in the Air Force, so we moved around a lot. My husband and I have spent a lot of time traveling and moving. You know looking for the proverbial "greener grass". As my husband says, "the grass may be greener on the other side, but you still have to mow it". How very right he is.

We have recently come to the conclusion that we are just are not meant to stay in one spot very long, we're resigned to being nomads. I have a wonderful husband, we have been married since January of 1995 and have three awesome children, two boys and one girl. Our daughter lives in Oregon and the boys in Utah. It is hard having them so far away. We talk on the phone, text and communicate via Facebook often. Love being as involved as possible in my kids' lives. Love hearing about the things they have accomplished, the people in their lives, the good and the bad. Once in a while, when we're talking they'll say something that lets we know they were watching and listening to us, when they were growing up. That we did something right along the way.

Thank you Jesus, that we didn't completely mess up our wonderful children. Being their parent has been and continues to be an incredible experience.

MANNA

Before I go any farther, let me explain what Manna is with reference to the Bible. Here are some verses from the Bible on 'manna'.

Then the lord said to Moses, "Behold, I am about to rain bread from heaven for you; and the people shall go out and gather a day's portion every day, that I test them, whether they will walk in my law, or not. *Exodus 16:4.* God says He is going to feed His beloved children. He has laid down some ground rules. He wants to see whether or not they will trust Him.

And Moses said, "Let no man leave any of it over till the morning. "But they did not listen to Moses. Some left part of it till morning, and it bred worms and stank. And Moses was angry with them." *Exodus 16:19-20.*

"and He rained down on them manna to eat and gave them the grain of heaven." *Psalm 78:24*

Wow, God Himself sent to his children bread from heaven so they would not be hungry. This manna would nourish and sustain them for 40 years as they wandered through the desert. There are many other references in the Bible to manna. I'm sure you get the idea.

Now the way I'm using 'Manna', is to refer to the things in our lives that God gives us, to feed and nourish us, physically, mentally and spiritually. The same as with the actual 'Manna' He gave the

Israelites. Things that God gives us to help us along on our journey through this life. Stumbling thru our own desert, trying to find the Promised Land. We are not meant to hold on to these things. It is only to feed and nourish us for a short time. We are to trust that God will provide for us.

This manna, can be anything. It maybe that job you love, the place you're living, your house, a friend. Manna can refer to material possessions or things less tangible. For you, it may be your skill set, the way you learned to do or view things or maybe it's that car you're driving. It can be anything that becomes more important to you than trusting in God. Hopefully, you get the idea, if not it should become clearer as you read this book.

Anything that God has given you and you are now attached to and refusing to let go of. Those things that have become more important than God, they cloud our judgment. These things have become your idols. Letting go of these things will help free you up to hear more clearly from God and receive the gifts He has waiting for you. Letting go of this 'manna' doesn't always mean giving away or throwing out, sometimes God just wants you to set things aside for a time, so He can give or teach you something new.

THERE AND BACK AGAIN

My family moved to Oregon from northern Michigan, about 10 years ago, after almost a year of my husband and I being separated (but that is another story). After God brought us back together and healed much of the brokenness in us, it was time for a fresh start. We set money from our taxes aside, set up a place for us to rent, and reserved a 24-foot moving truck; a few months in advance.

When the time came, we spent the day and night packing the moving truck, got a little sleep, got up finished packing, got ready, went to our friend's wedding (my husband was in the wedding party), and then headed for Oregon, all within, approximately 36 hours.

We did some planning, we didn't pray about it, at all. We were just going about our merry way, doing things in our time, in our way, big mistake. This would be the longest journey we had traveled together and God had some interesting adventures in store for us.

For starters, our eldest son (who was sixteen at the time), was not at all happy about the move. We were taking him away from his home and his friends. The friends, mind you, were being far from a good influence on him. Well, the two younger kids were just happy we were all a family again. This was a big new adventure, for them.

We had a cell phone that got no service for most of the trip from Michigan to Oregon, so we could not keep in touch with the new landlords. When we finally reached Oregon, days later, and were finally able to call our new landlords, we found out, that due to some unforeseen problems they had rented the place to someone else. There we were, my husband, I and our three children (one of which was a very unhappy teenager), a twenty-four-foot moving truck and nowhere to go. We were now thousands of miles from what we had once called home. Let me tell you that was a day I will never forget. Scared and with no idea how we would get through this, faith in God was all we had. God was making a little course correction for us; we, of course, had been heading down our own path. We had no idea what we would do or where we would go. Twenty-six hundred miles from home (Michigan), 3 children, a 24-foot moving truck and nowhere to go. Time to panic yet?

Thank God, my husband's younger brother lived not too far from where we were and was gracious enough to let us stay with him and his family. One problem solved. We still had a twenty-four-foot moving truck that we needed to unload and return. The trip had taken longer than planned already, the truck needed to be unpacked and turned into the company. We were on a time limit. We started searching through listings trying to find a place to rent, we checked out a few, to no avail. Then we found a listing about 50 miles away and decided to check it out. We looked at it and moved in the next day. We unloaded the truck and returned it, barely in time, thank you Jesus. Money was already going to be tight and neither of us even had lines on jobs yet. There we were, working on our plans, not even thinking to ask God for guidance or what His plans for us were. After quite few more trials and mishaps, (Can't imagine why, after all, we were following *our plans*) we got work going and things finally seemed to start going right for us. We were both working, the kids were in school, even my eldest seemed to be having a change of attitude, and all was right with the world. That's right, things were going **my way.**

Then, less than a year after moving to Oregon, I ended up in the hospital with meningitis, lost a week out of my life and almost died. Oh, did I forget to mention that my gallbladder almost exploded (it was so full of infection) and they had to do emergency surgery to remove it. Would love to say that there was some life-changing near death experience, not just a total blank, but that's all that was there a great big blank. An entire week of my life gone forever and my life had now turned upside down. Sent home with I.V. Antibiotics and still very much disoriented, I could barely remember my own name. Now completely deaf in my left ear and could barely walk across a room, just standing up was challenging. After a year of dealing with everything myself and being fairly independent, now almost, completely dependent on others and very afraid.

Answering the phone was an experience, after hearing nothing, and getting mad and frustrated I would hang up the phone. Who knows how many people got hung up on, before realizing I was putting the phone to my left ear. The one that was now totally deaf. Couldn't even leave the house by myself, because of my balance problems, you lose inner ear it doesn't just affect your hearing it destroys your balance as well. I won't even go into all of the long-term effects, of the (though seemingly minor) brain damage.

A mess, scared, very frustrated, very weak and with no idea if I would ever feel anything close to normal again, what was next, what did my future hold? God was using these things to begin teaching me some very valuable lessons. Like how to trust and lean on Him. After getting a cane and starting to push myself to get out of the house on my own, I started regaining some of what had been lost. Though scared to death, moving forward was the only option. My independence counted on it. Once again, I did not ask for help from Daddy, God. Oh, almost forgot to mention, driving was not an option, that's right, I took myself off the road. My mind was too scrambled to drive safely. This meant having to depend on others to get anywhere. We lived in a town of approximately nine hundred people, 30 miles away from the nearest city. We had a post office, a small grocery store and a handful of other small businesses. We didn't even have a stop light.

Walking all the time now, over to the post office, the store, taking my youngest to school and sometimes walking to the high school/middle school, a mile or so away was helping me regain my strength. Got to know that little town pretty well. A lot of people seemed to know me, the lady who walked everywhere. However, if I needed to go anywhere beyond the city limits, with my husband now working full time, thank God, I had to find someone to drive me. That at times, could be frustrating and very difficult. It is rather hard to plan things when you don't know how you're going to get there. You think if you plan far enough ahead, it shouldn't be that difficult. The fact is, some of the long term effects included memory loss. I was lucky to remember my own name, let alone planning anything very far ahead.

I had started going to church and was starting to learn a little. Still not sure of the exact time frame. Not sure if going to church or having meningitis came first. Some things, to this day, are still a bit of a jumble in my head.

Anyway, while sitting and watching a graduation, a few months after coming home from the hospital, things really hit me. By this time using a cane, got me from here to there and back. Watching a young lady walk up three steps, to receive her diploma, and not being able to comprehend how she could walk up those three steps without a cane, now that was pretty eye opening for me. It sounds pretty silly, but it just didn't make sense. That scared the daylights out of me. After all, I had walked my whole life without a cane. Why now, could I not understand how someone could walk up three steps, without one? That was a life changing moment for me. This had to change. This couldn't be what the rest of my life would be like.

Pushing myself even harder; walking at night and on surfaces that would be difficult for me to balance on, there had to be some glimmer of hope. It was helping, but not nearly enough for my taste.

It was about this time that some dear friends offered to help. A husband and wife, Kerry and Linda. They went to my church and were also strong in their Christian beliefs. They agreed to help me with the balance issues and regaining some of my strength. She was inspiring and encouraging. They would guide me and pray for and with me. They, however, would not let me slack and it would be up to me to do the hard work. They also told me that I needed to be praying and talking to God, asking for His help, healing and patience.

My husband and a group of guys that were in far better shape than me would be who I worked out with. That was pretty scary and intimidating. Working out with a bunch of big strong guys, and me barely able to walk across a room with my cane. They were, however, all very supportive and all good strong Christians. There was a prayer before every workout, we all took turns praying, and a lot of emotional support during. The thing that wasn't there was pity; no one was going to let me slack or feel sorry for myself, including my husband. There was a lot of hard work, a few tears and of course some self-pity, but through this, God was with me, strengthening me, holding my hand and guiding me forward. I am so very thankful that my dear friends, my loving husband and of course, most importantly, God did not give up on me. While still using my cane, I reentered the workforce. Then, after months of hard work, one week before starting a new job, I was able to give up my cane, permanently. Let me tell you, that was another very scary moment. The cane had been my security blank, my companion.

Approximately one week after giving up that cane, I started a new job. I could not have worked there, with the cane. Due to the nature of the work, the cane could have been used as a weapon against me and probably been seen as a weakness, to exploit, by the clients. The job would be working with people who had mental disorders and addictions, some of them straight off the street and going through withdrawals. This, eventually, leads me into working a full-time job, in the field I had wanted to be in, as long as I could remember, the psychiatric field.

Loved my job, loved my family, loved my church and loved living in a small town. These things were gifts from God, they were all wonderful, these things fed me in various ways, like the Manna God sent down to feed the children of Israel as they wandered in the desert. Manna is only meant to nourish for a time. We are not supposed to try to hold on to it. We are not supposed to try to save it. God wants us to show our faith by trusting that He will provide for us and let go of even the most awesome gifts, that He may give us even better gifts.

Well, needless to say, I was going to hold on to these gifts tightly, digging in my heels and was not going to budge. God graciously increased me in all areas of my life. I was growing spiritually, both as an individual and with my husband. God was showing me how miss informed I was and again gave me a course correction and

11

helped me start seeing things more through His eyes, instead of my distorted worldview. The world would say yes, hold on to that job, after all, it is something you have wanted for such a long time. Hold on to where you are, in a wonderful community, with great friends and an awesome church. Why let go of these things? Wow, was that an eye-opening time. Growing much closer to my church family and growing to love each one of them deeply. I had come a long way and was putting down roots, deep roots. I loved most everything about my life and was getting very comfortable.

My husband had started talking about moving elsewhere; of course from my perspective, that was not happening. The subject would get changed, maybe just ignored altogether. Other things were starting to unravel. No way, moving was out of the question. Things were finally going the way I wanted them to go and no one was going to change that.

God started talking to me; I had started learning about the Holy Spirit and had started listening to Him. He was telling me to start getting rid of some of the junk (material possessions) in my life. No idea why. Certainly, there would be no moving going on, anytime soon. Going through our stuff, getting rid of some things, that wasn't too hard, we had a lot of junk. Things that just weren't needed. Not really, trusting God to take care of my needs, my life had become very cluttered, gathered a lot of manna. You know, stuff that God tells us not to hold on to. Over the next year or so getting rid of stuff became pretty routine. Still not knowing why. I was comfortable and certainly had absolutely no intention of moving any time soon. It didn't matter if the house fell down around me. **I wasn't going to move!**

My husband had been talking about moving, the Holy Spirit had been nudging me and the house itself was making me physically ill. Black mold, multiple leaks, etc., etc. Like a strong willed, stubborn child having a temper tantrum, I absolutely was not going to budge. Then it happened. We got the call from our landlord that we would have to move and she would be sending us the written notice. They were going to move into the house, so we had to vacate. OK God, you win.

Throwing my hands up, we started looking for a new place, still wanting to stay in the area. Close to my kids' schools, driving distance from my work and close to my church. Do you see a pattern here? My, my all about me, me, me. I wasn't really thinking about my husband's wants or needs, wasn't really thinking about my children wants or needs and asking God what He wanted for me and my family, hadn't even crossed my mind. Once again, God started gently nudging me in the right direction, His direction. With only a couple of weeks to find a place and get moved, we found another house. God again provided for us. The house was better, the neighborhood was better, the neighbors were awesome. I was still advancing in my work, but other things were starting to fall apart. Remember what happens to Manna when you try to hold on to it. **"Notwithstanding, they hearkened not unto Moses; but some of**

them left it until morning, and it bred worms and stank". *Exodus 16:20 KJV*. Let me tell you, my life was starting to get pretty stinky.

God, being patient and loving, as He is, continued to nudge me. He stepped back and let me take my time, learning lessons that needed to be learned. He sat back keeping an eye on me, stumbling through doing things *my way*. I didn't want to move and didn't want things to change. Things were just fine the way they were. After all, change is never easy. In fact, sometimes change can be downright painful. It feels good living in those comfort zones. There, everything is familiar. There I didn't have to trust in anyone or anything else.

Me, important, one among billions (or more). Why should God bother with my petty problems? Knowing that really listening would mean, that God was going to tell me things were about to change. Maybe just ignoring Him would work, maybe holding on to things just the way they were for a while longer, wouldn't be noticed. Maybe, God would forget about me and I could stay right in the middle of my comfort zone, all warm and snug.

God does notice and takes the time to speak to me. He does this with me a lot, as He does with all his children, if only we choose to listen. That's the key, we have to be willing to listen and then follow His guidance. He, after all, He has nothing but good in store for us. *"I know the plans that I have for you, declares the Lord, plans for welfare and not for evil, to give you a future and a hope."* **Jeremiah 29:11 ESV.**

Wow, think of it, the Creator of the universe has personally made a plan for you. He has given attention to every detail. He has not left out anything, tailor made this plan for you and nobody else. He has worked out all the fine details and taken great care that all the provisions are in place. That my dear ones is how very much He loves and cares for you.

God gave us free will and He continues to let us make our own choices, even when we mess up. He can use even those mess ups to teach us new lessons. It's not that He wants us to stumble; He really would prefer to save us all the pain and suffering from all of our mistakes. God knows that the only way we can learn to truly love and trust Him, is if we have the right to choose of our own free will. He allows us to make our own mistakes. Love can never be forced or coerced. Real love, which is what God truly desires, has to be our choice.

A WALK THROUGH THE DESERT

"And the whole congregation of the children of Israel murmured against Moses and Aaron in the wilderness". <u>**Exodus 16:2.**</u> Well, we all tend to complain when our bellies are empty. We just cannot stand being hungry. When we ask God "Fill us, oh Lord", He loves us and does not wish us to remain hungry and complaining. It is truly difficult to think about much else when you're wandering around the desert with an empty belly. God already had a plan to feed His children, they only had to ask. God knew that His children would get hungry. He knew they would start to whine and complain. God would not bring His precious children out into the desert without a plan in place to take care of all of their needs. I mean what loving parent would toss the kids out in the middle of know where, with no food or provisions and expect them to wing it, all on their own. God is loving and had everything planned out. We as children cannot always see what lies ahead. We have to question everything. We have a hard time just believing that God's got our backs and knows what's best. We are stubborn, strong willed children. Fortunately for us, we have a loving, thoughtful Father, who has already made plans for us to prosper.

How often do we set out on our journeys totally unprepared, with no real forethought about what we may need along the way? We run out the door and halfway into the journey, realize that we need something that we could have brought with. Then to make it worse, we don't stop to ask the One who knows the way to get there. We're too proud to ask Daddy (Abba, Father), to help us. We are too busy trying to prove to the world, how smart and independent we are. Father really does "**know best**". Not only has He already got the whole journey planned out, so that you can get to your destination on time, while enjoying the sights along the way, He has wonderful surprises in store for you as well. He has drawn you out a detailed map, with easy to follow instruction (including landmarks to help you find your way); He has highlighted the route for you and left you supplies and special gifts and presents to make the journey more fun. We're in such a hurry to get where *we want to go*, that we crumble up the instructions and map without even looking at them, toss them aside and off we go on *our own* journey. Heaven knows we don't need any help. We have taken trips before, doing it all our own way. Completely forgetting all the trials, we had along the way. All the road blocks we ran into. Forgetting how many exciting things we wanted to do along the way, cool stops we planned to make, but we lost our way, and missed all the good stuff. We got off on the wrong road, which took us down a very tough bumpy road. It leads us into a very scary place and we had no idea how to find our way back. There we are stuck, alone and afraid and too darn proud to admit it.

Even well into our journey, if we would just stop and say "God, please help me", then wait for Him to answer, God (Abba, Father,

Daddy) would provide everything we need and set us carefully back on the right road. What God provides is not always what we expect or want, but it is what we need. More often than not if we look back on things from our past, we realize what we wanted at the time would have only made things worse. Like the song says, "You don't always get what you want, but if you try sometimes, you'll get what you need." More correctly, if you follow God's plan, in the first place, just maybe you won't get lost and miss out on all the good things along the way.

If asked, Father God would happily, send us a guide, to make sure we did not get lost and could enjoy the sights along the way. The fact is, He has already done that, in the form of 'Holy Spirit'. When Jesus went to be with his Father in heaven, He said **"It is expedient for you that I go away, for if I go not away, the Comforter will not come unto you; but if I depart, I will send Him unto you".** *JOHN 16:7 KJV*

The 'Holy Spirit", lives inside you (after you except Jesus). He is that "still small voice", you hear, telling you the right choices to make. The one we should listen to, but only to often choose to ignore. You see, the Holy Spirit will not force His will on you, even though He knows what is best. He tries to guide you in the right direction, but we still have freedom of choice. Good or bad, we have the right to ignore even the best advice. Unfortunately, that also means we have to deal with the consequences of those choices, good or bad. Blaming God, other people or our circumstances will not change the outcome of our choices. Yes, we need to fess up, ask forgiveness and own it. Remember, God is quick to forgive and slow to anger. He may even help pick us up and dust us off, but that doesn't mean you get off scott free. Life is real, our choices are real and the consequences are real. The only way to learn, is to accept it, own it and move forward, lesson learned.

OK, now we are out there in the desert, all we can see for miles around is sand and more sand. We're tired, our feet are sore and we appear to be totally lost. Oh, and did I forget to mention that our enemies are quickly riding up behind us on chariots and (it just gets better), there is a vast sea in front of us. Friends and family around us and we're trapped. Nowhere to run; nowhere to hide. What are we going to do? We really only have one choice, panic, freak out, yell and scream. Of course not, God knows exactly where we are and what is needed. He knows about our enemies and their chariots being pulled by mighty steeds and led by a crazed mad man. He only wants you to believe in Him, have faith and know He loves you dearly. If you were to realize how much He truly loves you, then you would know that He would never really let anything hurt you. Well, except for our own choices. Yep, there's that darn free will thing. Sometimes it can be very inconvenient, when we don't want to take any of the responsibility on ourselves. All the freedom, none of the consequences.

He already has your salvation planned out. All you have to do is believe and have faith and let Him do the rest.

Now that we're done yelling, screaming and totally freaking out, too tired to do anything, we turn our faces to God and say "Help, please save us. You are our only hope." God reaches down and parts the sea and you are able to walk across on dry land. Imagine that, you don't even have to walk on water; you don't have to get your feet wet. All you had to do was 'be still and wait on the Lord' and you didn't even do that well. Still He comes through; still He saves us from the enemy. Then it gets even better, He brings the Red Sea crashing down on them, totally demolishes the enemy and makes sure that you know your enemy cannot even follow. The sea that once blocked your path and seemed like such an impassable barrier is now between you and any remnant of the enemy. You are now completely safe and secure and you dance and sing praises of thanks.

Hold on, that's not all, even before the whole sea thing, **"And the Lord went before them by day in a pillar of cloud, to lead them the way; and by night in a pillar of fire, to give them light; to go by day and night." Exodus13:21 KJV,** to guide and protect them? How cool is that. God is standing by watching over and protecting you 24/7, 365 days a year, forever.

MONSTERS

God himself is our night light, shining brightly. He knows a lot of his children are afraid of the dark and he does not wish us to stumble and fall. He stands near providing us with light and protecting us from "things that go bump in the night". He shines His light down and chases away all the shadows in our lives, so that we can clearly see. Though we really don't have any right to fear the 'boogeyman man' or 'the monsters under the bed'. We are after all children and of course we know that children don't always think logically. Children let their minds wander and create in their minds the most outlandish scenarios.

When we choose to live in the darkness of this world, it can be a very scary place. In that darkness we live in, it is only too easy for Satan to whisper in our ear, telling us how that simple shadow is actually a great and terrible monster, with long claws and sharp fangs, ready to devour us. Satan tells us about the big nasty monsters hiding under our bed, ready to jump out and get us. The interesting part is that he usually first tempts us with great promises. He promises us wealth, power, comfort, anything our heart desires and then lures us into those dark and scary places. He promises wonderful adventure and great riches, anything to entice us as far away from God's path as possible. Into the dark places, as far from Gods wonderful light as possible. Satan knows exactly what to say.

21

He acts like our best friend, telling us how great we are and how we can handle everything all by ourselves. Then when he has led us as far away as he can, he starts telling us what a dark and lonely place we have gotten ourselves into, points out that we have managed to wander off the path into the deepest, darkest part of the forest. He starts to whisper to us about all the big frightening monsters lurking behind every tree and under every rock. He points to the growing shadows, making stories about what is making the shadows. We forget that what makes shadows is usually much, much smaller than the shadows themselves. We forget that shadows have no real power, they can't really hurt you. Since we had always lived in God's bright and shining light we had never before seen shadows. We couldn't possibly realize that not only can shadows not hurt us, because they have no substance, but what is making those scary shadows is probably more afraid of us than we are of it. That which casts the shadow is pretty small and really not scary at all. If we just call out and ask God to shine His light into our dark places, the shadows suddenly disappear and that which casts the shadow is left exposed for what it truly is. Something small and wimpy, that could never do you any harm at all. If you just turned towards it and said "Boo" it would probably run away with its tail between its legs.

When we get ourselves into those deep dark places in our lives, we need to call out for God. We need to remember that we are never too far away for Him to reach us. Again, like a child, we assume that God will be mad at us. That He can't possibly forgive us, let alone come, once again to our rescue. Surely, this time, we have really messed things up, not even God can fix this one. This is the mother of all mess ups and too big even for God. Are you kidding me, after all, He alone created the entire universe? Do you really think there is anything too big for the Creator to handle? There is nothing too difficult for God to do and you are His beloved child. He knows just how prone we are to make mistakes. He loves us dearly and wants us to ask for His help. He wants to wrap His loving arms around us and 'make it all better'. Stop trying to figure everything out yourself. Stop trying to handle everything on your own, just ask and He will answer. Remember the answer is not always what you expect, it is however always what is best, even if we may not see it that in the moment. How many times have you looked back on things you did months or even years ago and realized that things could have been much worse if they had gone the way you initially planned? God sees the whole picture, not just one little piece, He really does know what it best.

WHINING AND DINNING WITH GOD

Don't you find it somewhat ironic that the Bible talks repeatedly about the importance of fasting? Going for periods of time limiting what we allow ourselves to eat or not eating at all (which is what we normally think of when we hear the word fasting). The Bible also makes countless food references. Jesus refers to Himself as 'the bread of life", *JOHN 6:35, KJV*. He tells parables about vineyards, there are references to farms and orchards and banquets. God knows how important food is to us. It sustains life, it provides nutrition, it brings us together. Food is the centerpiece of most celebrations, holidays, birthdays, weddings, graduations. Let's face it, life revolves around what we eat, where and how we grow and harvest our food. Food keeps us alive and when we lose the proper perspective on it can make us sick and even kill us.

As important as food is to us, we don't have a problem denying ourselves food, that is when it is on our terms. Maybe we want to lose weight, maybe certain foods upset our stomach or maybe we're allergic to certain kinds of food, which of course can be extremely serious. But what happens when we find ourselves out in the middle of the proverbial desert with no food in sight. We forget that our God, the God that created the entire universe, that's right, everything; and has promised us He will provide for everything we could possibly need. He promises to provide for us in abundance. God

24

doesn't just throw us a few scraps once in a while. He wants us to be well nourished both physically and spiritually. Why do we, only to often, feel like we starving? Why do we feel weak and afraid? Well, because we don't want to eat our veggies. We don't like those veggies and besides, we just have to save room for dessert.

Father, God knows we need a well-balanced meal to help us grow up big and strong. As with a well-balanced meal, to feed and nourish our physical bodies; our spirits need to be well nourished. We need to get into the 'meat' of God's word. We need to read our Bibles and yes, do Bible study with others who are new Christians, some who have been walking the walk for a while and some that are very mature in their faith. By discussing and studying with others throughout different stages we end up becoming well rounded. We are feeding our spirits a well-balanced meal. No one person has all the answers and we not only learn from teachers, but also by teaching others as we grow in our own faith. That is why 'the church', (which refers not to the physical building, but to the community of believers), is so very important. If we just sit alone reading our Bibles, then it is only too easy to go off on some rabbit trail. We get sidetracked and distracted way too easily. We need others to help us stay on track, keep us on that narrow path and not go off and get lost in the vast desert of life. Even when you feel you don't have anything important to give, you never know when something you say, some perspective you have, may actually help someone else.

When we try to do it all by ourselves, it is too easy to stumble and without someone to help us back up, you may find yourself laying out there in that vast desert hurt and afraid far too long. Besides, that meal is usually so much more enjoyable when you have others to share it with.

Another part of that balanced meal is prayer. Prayer doesn't have to be something fancy or religious, just talk to God. Don't get me wrong, there is a time and a place for more formal prayers. One of the biggest reasons a lot of people don't pray more is because they just don't have time. Well, if you're alone in your car, going for a run, eating a meal alone, at your desk, any time of the day or night, God is always listening. Another reason I hear a lot, is "I don't know what to say." Just start talking, He wants to hear about everything. He wants to hear about your hopes and dreams, you can sing, you can yell, you joke. We all have our own unique way of communicating. He wants to know what frustrates and angers you. He doesn't mind when you vent, in fact, it is better to yell and scream at God, get things off your chest so to speak, than it is to yell and scream at a friend, a family member or even an acquaintance. It can be very hurtful when we yell, scream and blame others. Have it out with God first and then if it is necessary, when you're calmer let The Holy spirit guide you in talking to the person in question. Just remember to take the time to listen as well. Yes, listening is a part of praying. Don't forget that prayer can and many times should be a two-way street, a conversation. Talk, laugh, yell, ask questions, then stop and remember to listen for answers, reassurance, guidance and sometimes just a pat on the back, or maybe even a good old-fashioned belly laugh. When I'm praying, conversing this way I usually make sure I'm alone, so I don't bother anyone, but mostly so I can talk openly and candidly with God. Of course, there are other kinds of prayer, such as when you pray with someone and corporate prayer when you pray with a group. I find the more I talk with God, one on one, the easier it becomes praying in front and with others.

Oh, before I forget and no less important is the dessert. That would be the praise and worship. Sometimes we have dessert first, getting us ready for the rest of the meal. **"Make a joyful noise to the Lord, all the earth; break forth into joyous song and sing praises."** ***Psalm 98:4 ESV*** *"Let them praise His name with dancing, making melody to Him with tambourine and lyre!"* ***Psalm 149:3 ESV.***

Abba, Daddy, Father God loves to hear us sing and see us dance with joy for Him. Kind of like when my daughter and son had been spending a few months with their grandparents they brought them both home. While we were showing the kids their new room, in the new house, my three-year-old daughter broke into a heartfelt rendition of the "I love you" song from Barney (that big purple dinosaur). I can tell you there wasn't a dry eye in the place. Most parents love hearing their children sing and seeing them dance. It makes us smile, even if they can't hold a note.

Well, what happens when we skip the meal altogether. We get out there in the middle of that big scary desert and a short time later we are whining and complaining that we're hungry. We forget that God not only knows us, and what we need, He already had a plan in place long before our tummies started grumbling. He planted the garden in advance and harvested the crop and prepared the meal. **"Man did eat angel's food: he sent them eat to the full."** *Psalms 78:25. All* we have to do is sit down at the table and eat the wonderful meal God has prepared for us.

Throughout our lives, God feeds us in so very many ways, providing us with spiritual manna, filling our empty spirits. We try to hold on to this spiritual manna trying to save some for the next day. We'll just set a small amount aside for tomorrow, just in case God fails to follow through on His promises. Besides, everyone knows how much better day old bread is then a fresh wonderful feast God will set out for us the next day. God promises, *"I will never leave thee, nor forsake thee." Hebrews 13:5,* and that He will provide and care for what is His. Maybe we have forgotten that we are indeed His and He loves us dearly. Maybe someone left out that section in our Bible, you know the one where Jesus says, **"Consider the lilies of the field, how they grow; they toil not, neither do they spin. And yet I say unto you, that even Solomon in all his glory was not arrayed like one of these. Wherefore, if God so clothe the grass of the field, which today is, and tomorrow is cast into the oven, shall He not much more clothe you, O ye of little faith."** *Matthew 6:28-30 KJV.* We question and doubt that the Creator of the whole universe is capable of caring for His beloved. Maybe we don't think we're important enough for God to take the time to care for us. We tend to forget that we are God's cherished children and He loves us dearly. As flawed humans, we would not dream of letting our children go hungry, even if the child is not our own. We are God's children, adopted through the great sacrifice that Jesus made for us. Adopted means that God not only created us, He also chooses to love us. When you adopt you carefully pick out and choose that child.

When the Israelites tried to save just a little bit of manna for the next day, just in case, what happened to the manna. That's right, it spoiled, it got foul and nasty and bug ridden. The Bible says, **"and it bred worms and stank."** *Exodus 16:20.* Why did this happen? Was it because God forgot to add preservatives? Maybe it was because God was just getting a kick out of watching His children squirm. I think not. Would you play a mean-spirited joke like that on your kids or the neighbor's kids, of course, you wouldn't? So why would a loving God do something so mean spirited and cruel?

God, in fact, wants us to trust in Him. He wants us to learn faith. He wants to have an intimate relationship with us. That can only come out of trust and faith. It comes from us knowing in the depths of our souls that we can trust in God and that He loves us completely and totally and only wants what is best for us. He wants to see us succeed and be happy and joyful. The entirety of the Bible is God's love promises to us. It shows us how much He loves us and to what lengths He will go, to save us from the clutches of satan.

When we finally find our way to the table, which God Himself has prepared for us, by the way he also drew out a detailed map, with easy to follow instructions on how to get to the party and even has guides and someone waiting at the doors to welcome you in and escort you to your special reserved seat. When we finally stop stumbling around and take the Guide's hand, so He may lead us step by step. When we finally allow the One who has been waiting, ever so patiently, at the door for us, to show us to our very special reserved seat; when we finally take our seat at the Father's table, what do we do? Do we say "thank you", for all that He has done just for us. No, we start to unload on Him and complain about how long the road was, to get there. We whine about how rough the journey was. How rough and rocky the road was and how sore our feet are. Never mind that the Father's Son personally washed us clean, spotless. Never mind the fact that we were allowed to drink deeply from the River of Life and be eternally refreshed. Never mind the Mountains God; Himself carried us over, leaving Him (Jesus), broken, bleeding and scarred.

Do we take even just a moment to say "Thanks, Dad"? You gave up so much for me. So much that I could be here with you at your table, which by the way you filled just for me with awesome abundance. What most of us do when we arrive, when we join our Father (who, has been waiting with anticipation for you) at his table, start to blurt out a long list of complaints. Think about it, if someone you know and love, someone you have invited to your home, someone whom you have spent a lot of time and effort preparing for. You tend to even the smallest detail so that everything could be just right for them. You have even sent your servants out to make sure they got there safe and sound. And when that did not work you sent out your most precious, your one and only Son to get them there, safe and on time and made them your most honored guests. Instead of being happy and thankful, they plop down at your table and proceed to tell you about how long and treacherous their journey was. They complain how tired they are, not once thanking you for the multitude of servants you sent out for them. The provisions you set along the road so that they would not starve, provisions so they would not be thirsty. This guest leans over to the One sitting next to him (Jesus, God 's one and only Son, the One that guided you there) murmurs something about getting lost repeatedly along the way, not once being thankful for His guidance. Not once admitting that, in fact, the Guide was not only very familiar with the territory, but that He had risked life and limb desperately trying to show you down the right path. Even came to chase after you, when you decided to go off on some rabbit trail. He ran after you to stop you from running, headlong towards a jagged cliff and where you could have fallen to your demise. You would think after all Father God has done for us that we would be at least a little bit grateful. After everything He has done for us, we should be singing His praises and jumping up and down for joy. All we seem to be able to think about is 'me, me, me'. How I have been uncomfortable, tired, hungry, etc, etc, etc..

Think about those wonderful family gatherings. If it happens to be at your house, you spend your time days, weeks, maybe even months in advance preparing for your guests. Your family and loved ones. You want everything to be just right. You get out the good dishes, the linens that you set aside for a special occasion, maybe even go buy brand new stuff just for this big event. You plan games and outings. You buy food, especially for this gathering. You plan every detail. Then the big day arrives and the guests start arriving. As they come through the door, they start complaining about the crazy traffic, the horrible weather, how tired they are, how long the trip was. They don't seem to notice all the hard work you've done preparing for their arrival. They don't mention the wonderful smells coming from the kitchen. They don't even seem to care about your warm smile and loving embrace they received when they arrived. Then to make it worse Aunt Minnie doesn't like the way cousin George is dressed. Joe's wife doesn't like the snacks you set out because she's on a diet and now it's your fault that her dress isn't going to fit right. Wow, not so much as a thank you. How would that make you feel. That is what we do to God all the time. He has planned out every detail. He wants nothing but the best for us, yet we complain and blame Him when things go haywire. We act like our poor choices are all His fault. We act like everything that is wrong with the world, is wrong because God is mean, hateful and vindictive. In fact, God loves us more than we can possibly imagine.

That is why He allows us to make our own decisions, good or bad. You cannot truly love if you cannot make that choice for yourself. Likewise, everyone has the right to make their own decision good or bad. We also have to remember that we also must deal with the consequences of those decisions. God has provided a path back to Him and all the blessings He has waiting for us. That doesn't mean we will not have to pay the price due for our mistakes (His son Jesus paid that enormous price for our salvation), we will however still have consequences to our actions.

WHO'S AFRAID OF A BULLY

Satan, the one that will do anything he can to hurt GOD, knows that he can do nothing, to directly hurt God. This means he has to find a less direct route to take. He knows that by going after what God loves most, he can hurt God. Satan will deceive and manipulate us, God's children, anyway he can. He wants to lure us as far away from the Father's loving embrace as possible. He wants to separate us from God and cause us to run straight down into the fiery depths of hell with him. Remember that misery loves company. Please remember also, that when one of God's children turn away from Him or choose not to believe in Him, this breaks His heart. This is the true aim of the devil. By causing us to choose to be separated from our Heavenly Father, the devil's aiming his flaming arrows straight into the heart of the Father who so dearly loves us. Even in this regard, the devil proves himself to be a true bully. He does not attack us for our sake, but in the attempt to hurt the Creator. The devil will lie to us, telling us how important he thinks we are, when in fact to him we are no more than a simple pawn in his game.

What we seem to forget is that Father God values us greatly. He as a loving parent, is not willing to lose anyone of His precious children. He seeks us, He pursues us. However, if we choose to keep turning away and taking our own path, the one that leads us straight to hell, He will allow us that choice. We are not dragged into hell against our will. We run there, headlong through the gates and dive in. No one is there but by their choice.

Like any bully and of course satan is the master of all bullies, he likes to intimidate and degrade us. He wants us to believe that we are not tough enough, not strong enough to stand up to him. You know what, he's right. By ourselves, there is no way on earth that we have what it takes to defeat our enemy. We just cannot take him on all by ourselves. That's OK, though, because we have a Big Brother that is stronger, tougher and smarter by far than that old bully, the devil. That's right Jesus. If that were not enough Father God is standing right behind us whenever we need Him.

The thing we tend to forget about bullies, is usually the reason they're being a bully in the first place, is because they're afraid. They know the only way they can get 'respect', is by making others afraid of them. They usually pick on someone that is smaller and weaker than they are and then make a big show of picking that smaller weaker person. Sometimes they will start rumors about the other person or even spread rumors about how big and tough they are. Something along the lines of, "I heard he beat up the biggest guy on the football team." or "I heard he took on 10 guys, single-handedly." We all know that once a rumor starts it just keep growing.

So it begins. We hear these outlandish rumors, but because other people say it, it must be true. Then here he comes, right in our directions, he is pretty big and everyone says how tough and mean he is, so we try to run away or hide or both. We don't want to go running to Big Brother (Jesus) and Daddy (Father, God), what will everyone think, we don't want everyone to think that we afraid. We want Big Brother and dear old Dad to be proud of how we can handle it all by ourselves. You figure if you stay out of his way, he won't want to beat you up. Guess what, he knows who your Daddy is and he's jealous and that makes him mad. He knows that your Dad loves you and wants to give you all the best stuff so now it's all your fault that he's miserable and he is going to go out of his way to make you pay, he knows you won't go running to Daddy or even your Big Brother, because you can handle it all by yourself.

How often do we do the most foolish things, just to prove how mature and tough we are? Deep down we know we need help. We won't even turn to friends (other Christians), who would come running in a heartbeat if we would just ask. That's what we're supposed to do, support and help each other.

No, we're too proud and too bull-headed. What do we do, we give the bully (satan), exactly what he wants? Ourselves, served up on a silver platter. We might as well put a giant bulls eye in the middle of our face and say there, see if you can hit that. Well, of course, he's going to take you up the that offer. Big Brother and dear old Dad can only stand back watching, because you want to do it all by yourself. Why do we think we can and have to handle everything all by yourself? We have great resources and we decide not to use them, not to call on the one who would happily step in and make everything better. He would step in between you and that awful bully and put a stop to it all. Not to mention that when the other 'kids' see how much your Dad (Father, God) loves you, maybe they would do the same.

Do you really think that you're the only one the bully has been terrorizing? Of course not. That's the nature of a bully, the more people they can terrorize the more powerful they feel. You ask for help and band together and suddenly they turn into a big fat wimp. If satan is using another person to bully you, then maybe, just maybe when they see how much you are loved, that person may just want to change. When they see that God and Jesus really do want to help you and how much you have changed because of that unending love and grace, that may be just what they need to accept the wonderful free gift of grace. Let's face it, as the Bible says, **"for all have sinned and fallen short of the glory of God".** *__Romans 3:23.__* They may just want to experience the love and kindness that they see you receiving. They may never have known that feeling before. Remember, satan, the master of all bullies, has probably been tormenting them as well. Pray for them and ask God to help you show them God's infinite love and grace. Be careful and be wise, ask God to guide you. You may only be the first domino in their life that will start them on the road to true change or you may be the last straw that breaks through and shows them the awesome light of God, to shine love and warmth in the darkness that has been their life.

There was a situation I found myself in a few years ago. While working at a psychiatric facility, there was a coworker that just seemed to have it in for me. We had a lot of problems getting along. It got bad enough that I actually went to my boss and asked if she could step in and do something to help with this situation. Shortly after walking out of the office, I had a change of heart, turned around and told my boss not to worry about it. I said that prayer was going to be the route I would take. She agreed to wait and see what would happen. That is exactly what was needed to change things. After months of not being able to stand even being in the same building with this particular coworker, and shortly after Praying about the situation, things began to change. Not to say that we became best friends, but the change was very dramatic. We started getting along very well. Actually had good conversations and enjoyed each other's company. Wow, after all of that time, now to be on good terms with her was amazing. The only explanation for this fairly sudden and dramatic change was God stepping in and changing both of our hearts. This was not the only time this happened. There was another coworker I was having issues with as well and again prayer was the turning point. Laying it down at the feet of God and letting Him take hold and change both of us.

Sometimes we just have to be willing to set aside our pride and let God change us from the inside out. Could not tell you exactly what changed or how, only that it was thanks to God that everything got so much better. This all happened within about two weeks, after months of me pulling my hair out trying everything I could, to change things myself. Both of these coworkers quickly become people I very much respected, enjoyed working with and being around.

WHAT GOD HAS COOKING

We go through life trying to collect and save things. We collect clothes, furniture, cars, tools, nick knacks, degrees and even friends. The object is to see how much stuff we collect, "he who dies with the most stuff wins", or at least that is what the world tells us. Any of the many things in our lives, that we collect and hold on to, can be our manna. Things that in many cases just weigh us down and keep us wandering aimlessly in the desert. God gives us things that will nourish and sustain us. Then we begin to cling to them, afraid if we let go, there will never be anything else, no more manna. We gather these things unto us and tuck them away in a safe place, just in case when tomorrow comes there is no more new manna. Then we can go back to pull them out, because we are too impatient and afraid to believe (and we just must have them now) only to find that what once gave us sustenance is now spoiled and foul. These things no longer bring us joy; they no longer fill and nourish us. In fact, now these things that we have collected and carefully stored away, against God's commands, make us sick, tie us down and keep us from being able to move forward and finally finding our proverbial promised land. Remember the Israelites journey should have only lasted a short time.

I recently had this happen in my own life. About a year or so ago I bought a used Jeep, a Grand Cherokee. It wasn't perfect, but it was mine and I really liked my Jeep. We were going through some changes and decided to sell it. My niece found out I was selling it and asked if she could buy it from me. We both tried to convince her not to buy it. We told her the things we knew were wrong with it and that it would need work done before it was really safe to drive in northern Michigan winter. She insisted on buying the jeep and we reluctantly agreed. Well the Jeep that had been such a blessing for me, turned out to be a nightmare for my niece. After a few months and it stranding her multiple times and putting more money into it than she had planned, she decided to give it back. We were in Alabama at the time, so I told her would come get it as soon as we could, when we got back to Michigan. Figuring that we would see what was wrong with it, maybe fix it up and I would have my jeep back. Worst case scenario we could sell it and get something else.

When we got back, we ran into some complications, so we were unable to make the 2-hour drive to go get the Jeep. She, in turn, said she could bring it to the junkyard and send me the cash (which mind you would have helped both her and I, at that time). No, I insisted on getting the Jeep and told her we would come get it as soon as we could. Over the next couple weeks' tension started to build between us, but I was still insisting on holding on to the Jeep (my manna). Finally, her uncle, that she was staying with, said it had to go. He wanted it out of his yard. I still insisted I would try to go get the Jeep. Finally realizing that it was driving a wedge between me and this niece, I so loved, I told her to go ahead and send it to the junkyard. I'm in the process of writing this book about not clinging to things and what was I doing, that's right, trying to 'Save the manna". Tell you what, it was getting pretty stinky. God has always provided for us, in the most incredible ways. Time to take my own advice. Yes, even someone like me, maybe, especially me, has to be reminded, "Don't save the manna".

God provides us with the manna and has promised us that He will give us fresh manna daily. He provides us with all the good things in our lives that we need. All He asks in return is that we trust in Him and believe in His promises. DON'T SAVE THE MANNA. He will give us more, fresh, new manna tomorrow. We don't have to hold on to the moldy old manna from yesterday. It will only make us sick and keep us from moving forward.

God does not want us to depend on things or even people in our lives. That does not mean that it is bad to have friends and family around us. We were in fact made to need each other. It does not mean that we should not strive to better ourselves. It only means that God wants to have faith that He the *Maker of Heaven and Earth,* absolutely can and will care for His beloved creation. That is us, you and me. *He* wants to us to understand that as a loving Father, He wants us to be happy, He wants to pour out His great abundance upon us, He wants to bless us.

I heard a very wise lady say once "When God gives you a test, you can't fail them, He just keeps giving them to you till you get it right."

40 years wandering in the desert that is a lot of retakes. God, help us to get the test right the first time so that we can move on. Oh, and by the way, these are all open book tests. We can open our Bibles up any time for the answers; in fact, Father, God encourages us to do just that. We can even ask for help from the Holy Spirit and other Christians.

As time goes on and I learn more and more about God, learning to hand more things over to God. For instance, having done a lot of cooking since I was a kid, and getting compliments on my cooking, and lately more and more successes than ever in the kitchen. Things that have never turned out exactly right are turning out wonderfully. I also find that my time in the kitchen is more joyful and a lot less stressful. While in the kitchen, God uses the time to teach me things. Mostly to lean on Him, not on the counter. Sometimes the simplest things can become great lessons. Adding a bit more spice to the cake, can be a lesson about how God intends our lives to be a bit spicier, more fun and exciting. How taking the time to turn down the heat on the stove a bit, can become a lesson on what slowing down a bit and listening to what God is trying to tell me, will help things simmer just right and not boil all over the place. Ever notice that when we get in too much of hurry our lives seem to boil over and we not only get burned, but things take a lot longer because we have to stop and clean up the mess we created. If we had followed God's recipe book in the first place, i.e. the Bible, things would have turned out much better and without the mess. That's always been a tough one for me. See, I'm one of those people that just can't stick to a recipe. Even boxed macaroni and cheese, well you guessed it, I have to change it, just have to do it my way. A lot of us, myself included, know what God wants, we know what the Bible says, but we just have to change it a little. We just know it will be better the way we want to do it. Of course, the good old tried and true recipes that have worked so well for years, can't possibly be as good as our latest idea. God is, however, the master chef. He wrote the cookbook and his recipes are perfect and if we would just learn to follow them, maybe the cake wouldn't fall and maybe the meat wouldn't burn. Just maybe His recipe for our life is just what we need after all.

Now, when getting ready to start something in the kitchen, I say something along the lines of, "OK God it's all yours. You know more than me", take a deep breath and do my best to listen to God's instructions. Undoubtedly, He will tell me to add a little bit of this, leave out that or maybe don't cook it quite so long, it's done take it off the burner. It's nice having a master chef with me in the kitchen and in my life. It's fun cooking things up with God. I have been absolutely amazed at some of the recipes that have, after all these years, finally turned out right. My family has noticed the difference as well.

Halleluiah, praise God. For the first time ever, my bread and cinnamon rolls turned out pretty darn good. I was so pleased when they turned out not just edible, but pretty tasty. That may sound silly to you, however, to someone, like me, who loves to cook and can make almost anything, never being able to have bread turn out right for me has been a great frustration. I have been talking to God about it and he told me to trust and listen. Well, of course, as always, He was faithful. With God's help, making these things was no longer, a big frustration for me. Imagine for the first time at age 46, considering I've been cooking since I was a kid. Like with the bread, if I had learned to listen sooner and trust in God, imagine how much different things in my life might be. *But he answered, "It is written, Man shall not live by bread alone, but by every word that comes out of the mouth of God". Matthew 4:4.*

What an incredible way for God to teach me yet another lesson. For me, the kitchen is turning into a classroom and I never know what new and exciting things God is going to teach me while in the kitchen. God created each one of us and He knows how to speak our language. He is really good at stirring the pot, so to speak. That extra dash of salt might be His leading into how we are the salt of the earth; the pot that just boiled over might be His way of telling us that, something in our lives have reached the boiling point because we were in too much of a hurry to just get it done. If instead we would just turn down the heat and let it simmer. Things would turn out much better and we wouldn't have such a mess to clean up afterward. Not to mention, we could then have some time while the pot is simmering, to relax or get something else done. After all is said and done, it's all in Gods very strong, loving and capable hands, if we can only follow His recipe. His recipe for our life has a wonderful flavor and aroma. Some of the ingredients, to us, may seem a little odd. We just know that couldn't possibly work, but He has already tasted the finished product and it is wonderful. If we can learn to follow the recipe the way he made it, remember this is coming from someone who just has to change boxed mac and cheese, then just maybe things will turn out the way He has it planned. Oh, what a glorious plan He has for each of us.

We, yes, I am including myself in that, just need to learn to trust and have an ounce of faith. Jesus said **"Because you have little faith,"** **he said. "I assure you that if you have faith the size of a mustard** **seed, you could say to this mountain, 'Go from here to there,'** **and it will go. There will be nothing you cannot do".** _**Matthew**_ _**17:20 CEB.**_ That little tiny mustard seed produces a large plant. Who would have thought that something so small as a grain of sand could grow into something so big? Oh, and about that mountain, what to us is this enormous mountain to God is no more than a grain of sand. How hard is it to move a grain of sand?

One of the points here is that God knows you; He knows what we need and how to get us to understand on our level. He knows how we learn. You and I, have to be willing to listen and do our part. If we decide to go off on our own road, do things our own way and ignore what God is telling us, He will let you. He, after all, did give us all, free will. When things fall apart and don't go the way you want them to, don't blame God. Take a good long look at yourself and take responsibility for your own actions. Own your decisions and their outcomes. If I'm cooking something in the kitchen and decide to turn the burner on and then walk way and forget about, who is responsible for the boil over or burnt pan? That's right, me. It wasn't my son, who just happened to walk into the kitchen and find the pan boiling all over the stove or smoldering and ready to catch fire. It wasn't the electric company that provides the power for the stove to work. It wasn't even the stoves fault; it was just doing what it was made to do. I'm the one who turned it on and walked away and forgot about it. I'm the only one to blame, that's right, ME. It's my mess and I am responsible for cleaning it up. You know, however, if you ask and are truly repentant of what you've done God may still help you clean up that big mess you just made.

God has also blessed us with a garden. I prayed over the land before my husband started to work the ground. I prayed again as my husband was working the ground. We prayed over the plants and seeds before planting them and as we put them in the ground. We prayed throughout the time of growing. Yes, my wonderful husband has prayed over the garden as well. You say that seems like an awful lot of praying. Prayer is our strongest weapon against the enemy. So, why wouldn't we want to pray over our garden, our families, our schools, churches and of course our government. We pray to ask for God's guidance, His healing, His protection. We have had a great abundance with our garden, this our first year on this property. It's a house with seven acres, a chicken coop, a 2 car garage and a barn (I love the barn) and the garden is 200 feet by 60 feet. We have been harvesting for the last couple months and Oh, what a harvest. We have had corn, beets, beans, squash, lettuce, tomatoes and much more. We have been freezing and canning and we have been able to give a lot away. On top of what we have grown ourselves, we have been able to harvest wild grapes at one of my husband's fishing spots. We also ran into someone my husband and I both know who has orchards. My husband was talking with him and he said that he was downsizing the orchards and we could pick as many cherries as we wanted from the small orchard, they weren't using. We barely scratched the surface and we brought home 15 gallons and gave away almost as many. We have been praising and thanking God a lot and have been eating very well.

There have only been a few things we have had to buy. One week though, we were running shy on milk and eggs and had no money to get any. That night when my husband came home from work, he brought with him 3 gallons of milk and two 18 packs of eggs. A guest where he worked, had left behind milk and eggs and he was able to bring them home or he would have had to throw them out. Halleluiah, praise God. Why God chooses to bless us so greatly in this way, well maybe it's because He knows that not only will we be thankful, He knows we also enjoy using this abundance to help others. Why God chooses to bless someone one way and not another, only He truly knows.

The neighbors wanted to have chickens for eggs, but did not have a chicken coop. We had a chicken coop and did not have the money to get the birds. We let them use the coop and in return, we were given eggs. Again, Halleluiah, praise God. We have been determined to utilize as fully as we can what God has so blessed us with and things are unfolding in some pretty amazing ways. I don't know what else God has on the menu. We have only had the first couple of courses and there is much more to come. The table is set and God has prepared an amazing meal for us, we only need to be willing to sit at his table and partake with Him. We are not asked to sit alone and eat a cold tasteless meal. God is at the table that Jesus prepared and the Holy Spirit has whipped up a magnificent multi course meal for us to enjoy together. Food, family and fellowship. While we're at it, why not invite all our friends and neighbors and make it a real party. The more the merrier.

Just think of what it would be like, if more people would follow God's plan. If more people would tithe not just on money, but those who have gardens and farms were to tithe 10 percent of their harvest, I would bet hunger issues would go away. People would not go without food. Especially in this great nation, where we have so much and throw so much away. In fact, I would guess there would be an overflow. Wow, what an amazing thought, a world without hunger, the way God meant it to be.

The more I follow God's plan, the more I do as he leads, the more blessed I become. This is so for all of God's children. How very amazing is Gods abundant Love. He has thought of everything, because He loves us so very much. He wants us to trust Him and believe that He has our best interest at heart. Even in the midst of our darkest moments God knows what we need and how things will work out best for us.

GOD'S GREAT GIFTS

As a child standing fast, arms overloaded with presents and Daddy saying, "There is still more. I have even more and better gifts." First, however, you need to set down and set aside the presents in your arms that you are holding on to.

As a child with new toys, we grasp tightly to what we already hold in our arms. Those wonderful gifts that you have barely had a chance to play with. Those wonderful and exciting new toys. We just don't understand that in order to receive the rest of what God has for us, we must first be willing to set down (for a time), what we have already received. We hold fast, we dig in our heels and refuse to let go. Even with the promise of yet greater and more wonderful gifts.

With our arms already full, we are not able to receive more of what God has for us. We know that what we already have is wonderful and we have scarcely had a chance to play with our wonderful new toys, and understand what they can do and how they work. How could anything be better and why should we have to give up what we have just received. That's the point; God isn't asking us to give up anything. He doesn't expect us to give back the gifts He has already given us. He, just wants us to set them down for a while, so that our arms are empty to receive new gifts. God does not break His promises; God does not take back what he has given. God does,

51

however, want to lavish many, many gifts and blessings upon you. You are His beloved, his dear ones. Good fathers enjoy giving to their children and watching them light up when daddy makes time for them.

God is the best Daddy you could ever imagine. He gives us gifts beyond imagination. He disciplines only out of deep and unending love for us. There is never malice or any intent to in any way, harm us. He disciplines with the sole intent of correcting our mistakes so that we can, in fact, become the best us possible.

I one day, a number of years ago, had spent the day fighting with my eldest child. He was at that time a teenager and well, need I say more. Frustrated and angry, sitting in a dark room alone, crying and shaking, not knowing what else I could possibly do with my son, when God as always gave me a revelation that shook me to my core (as these revelations always do). Broken and weeping the only thing I could do was to tell God how very sorry I was and suddenly my day long battle seemed very small and my love for Him seemed very big. What was this revelation, well, quite simply that I had been fighting with one child and that God has a whole world full of His children and that we are all spoiled children. Sitting there weeping, crying out "God, I am so sorry, so very sorry. I am dealing with one and you have the whole world and we're all spoiled children." What an incredible thing for God in His infinite mercy to show me. He did this in such a loving and wonderful way and made it simple and yet so complex. He put it terms for me to easily understand.

These are part of the gifts that God gives us, to become the tools for us to use. We, like a certain tool man on a TV sitcom, can have all the best tools in the world. Tools with "more power" but if you don't know how to use them you just fumble around like a fool looking pretty ridiculous and you don't even know how ridiculous you are. Someone tries to step in and explain how to use these awesome new tools (i.e. the gifts of the spirit) and we just brush him off and sometimes even end up getting hurt or hurting those around us.

He's given us the best tools, they come with an instruction guide (the Bible) and He even throws in the best assistant in the world, The Holy Spirit. What do we do; we grab up the tools, toss aside the instruction manual (in case you missed it the instruction book is the Bible) and totally ignore the awesome assistant He has given us. Away we go, head strong, know it all's. God sits back, crosses his arms and says "Have at it. I'll be sitting right here when you decide you need me." We fumble around, trying to look like we know what we're doing, which after all our hard work with these wonderful new tools, we watch as our project falls apart or maybe even blows up. Amazingly enough, we are completely dumbfounded, since we obviously are experts in the field and know absolutely everything. You know the most amazing part is that God, Jesus, and the Holy Spirit are still patiently waiting for you to say, "I could use a hand here". They don't even get mad and turn away at the edge of sarcasm you have just used. They don't return the sarcasm or rub it in. He will also put it to you in terms you can understand. With me,

He knows that I am a very visual person. After all, He did make me and you, all of us so He knows the way we learn. God gives me very vivid images. It is not in ten different languages and you just have to find one that you can understand. He has hand made the tools, especially for you and put in terms that you can understand and in case that is not enough, don't forget the awesome Assistant that will not only help with whatever you need, He will make you look like an expert while doing it. We should remember, instead of getting a swelled head over what God has helped us accomplished, to give Him the credit. That way, when someone comes to us in amazement over what we just did, instead of having to try to continue making ourselves look good, we can just simply point back to God. We can let others know how great He is. You don't have to be the best everything to everyone, you only need to point to the One who truly does know all the answer. This is a much lighter load to bear. Maybe that is why Jesus said, "For my yoke is easy and my burden is light." **Matthew 11:30 KJV.**

HAPPILY, EVER AFTER

He has already written our "Happily ever after". So why can't we see it, why is it so very far away? A little tiny pin point of light, at the end of a very long tunnel?

Think about any fairy tale. They don't exactly start with a happy ending. If they did, the happy ending wouldn't mean nearly as much. What would be the point, if everything is already perfect, we really wouldn't need the life lessons. We wouldn't even need a knight in shining armor, a Savior.

First, we have to go through the tough stuff. You have to deal with the wicked stepmother, the trolls under the bridge, the fire-breathing dragon, and the deep dark forest. Your knight in shining armor, your prince charming, has to come to your rescue.

Through our many trials, we do not only learn and grow stronger and wiser, but we also learn who to trust in and depend on our Knight in shining armor. Who we are and what our strengths are, well, that's something we have to learn along the way. We learn what happens when we take off on some rabbit trail and fall down a deep dark hole. We have to find out what is really real and what is make-believe. That which we imagine can be even scarier than what is real.

Being afraid of the dark, most of the time that doesn't mean we are actually afraid of the absence of light. What we're really afraid of, is what we can't see. The unknown can be pretty scary. All we have to draw on are our past experiences. I don't know about you but I have had some pretty terrible past experiences. Things I would not wish on anybody. If we're not drawing on past experiences, we're listening to what the world has to say. The world is a pretty crazy, mixed up place, kind of like 'wonderland' and if we're relying on the world views of things, then what we are going to see may be a bit skewed, distorted and out of balance. It is no wonder we're so afraid of our own shadows. Those things that go bump in the night. The creaking door, the branch scraping across the window pane, the wind howling through the trees. They're all so much scarier in the darkness. We tend to fear what we do not understand, what we cannot clearly see.

Wandering through life's dark forest can be pretty darn unnerving and downright dangerous without a guide or at least a few landmarks. We seem to keep going in circles. Surely something must be devouring the trail of bread crumbles, we left behind us and maybe it's looking to devour us too. We have not only forgotten what path to take, I think we have even forgotten how to open and read the guide book. The Bible spells it out and if we will just ask God, He will make it clear and show us the right parts of His guide book at the right times in our lives. God has given us tutors and translators to help us. We have pastors, Bible studies, small groups and good Christian friends and neighbors. Those with more training, more life experience and a better understanding. God puts people in our lives for a reason. He knows we need help. You wouldn't give a college textbook to a kindergartener and expect them to understand it, though they may have fun coloring on the pages or tearing pages out to make paper airplanes. The books true meaning would not even be a mystery, considering we have not yet learned to read, heck we don't even recognize letters yet, we are (a lot of us) baby Christians. Is it any wonder that so many of us any baby Christians or maybe you haven't even been *born again* yet, can't understand God's instruction book for us, The Bible. It is hard to take an interest in something that looks like a bunch of incomprehensible chicken scratch on paper, which would be so much more fun to color our own picture on those pages, fill in our own stories.

Anyway, back to the deep, dark forest. Oh, did you really think we got out of there that easy.

When you are lost and all alone in life's deep, dark forest, everything seems menacing and threatening. We hear a twig snap and we imagine it's some great ferocious creature, coming, wailing through the trees to attack us. We hear the wind howling and we imagine yet another gigantic monster coming to devour us. Maybe there is only silence, so we imagine something nasty, creepy, crawly thing slithering up behind us to bite us with its venomous fangs to leave us writhing in pain, to die an agonizing death all alone in our deep dark forest. What we forget is that Father God knows every square inch of the forest and with His Glorious light shining throughout it is not only, not at all scary, in fact, it is quite beautiful.

Satan knows that we are frightened little children and the farther he can get us away from Daddy, from God's wondrous light, the easier it is to get us going down the wrong path, deeper into that dark scary forest with all those scary sounds and shadows and things that go bump in the dark. The darkness makes it hard to see where the true path is. We stumble along trying to find *our* way home and end up falling down the proverbial rabbit hole. If you have ever read or have seen *"Alice in Wonderland'*, then you know what comes next. Things get pretty weird, everything seems to get turned upside down. Every once in a while we get a glance at that white rabbit running past, but instead of truly trying to follow him, we keep running headlong down *our own* path, trying to find *our own* way. If truth be known that white rabbit, our Savior Jesus, is searching desperately for us trying to save us. He is right there, close by all the time. He reaches out to us and we turn and run the other direction. Sure, this is a scary place, but we might miss out on some fun, something exciting. If we listen to Daddy and do as He tells us, surely we will miss out on all the excitement.

To use another well-known story, do you remember in *"Pinocchio"*, when he once again did not listen to Jiminy Cricket and went off to the carnival 'to have fun' with all the other children. He could do anything he wanted for as long as he wanted. What happened to him, he began to change into a donkey (yes, I know there is a more descriptive word for donkey, but well you can fill that in). Anyway, he started to turn into what he was being. Have you looked at yourself in the mirror lately, have you taken a long look at what you have become or are becoming? If you don't like what you see, it's not too late to turn back to God and let Him wash away all the bad stuff and make you back into His glorious image. He can make you something even more splendid than you can imagine. How much would most people pay for that kind of a makeover, and this is totally free, a gift, just because He loves you so very much. Kind of like when Pinocchio became a 'real boy', when the princess kissed the frog and he turned back into a prince or when the beast from "Beauty and the Beast" was turned back into a prince.

Remember first they had to go through some trials. They had a lot to learn before they became what they were truly supposed to be. They were, in fact chained to what they had become, enslaved by their bad choices. Since they were not willing to admit that it was their own decisions that were holding them in bondage, they could not break free from those heavy chains. We can be a lot like that, locked in a jail cell of our own making, key in hand, unwilling to open the doors to our cage. If we do that then we may have to admit that we messed up. Admit that we're not perfect. It's just easier to stay safely tucked away in our little cage.

THE GOOD OLE DAYS

How many of us look back on "the good ole days", and think those were "good times", completely forgetting what it was really like? Remember how the 'children of Israel', as soon as things got a little bit tough out in the desert, started complaining to God. They complained, *"Oh God, you have brought us forth into the wilderness, to kill this whole assembly with hunger." <u>Exodus 16:3.</u>* *They* complained and basically said, things may not have perfect back there in Egypt, but at least our bellies were full. Really, in Egypt they were slaves. They were forced to work long, grueling hours. They were beaten regularly and the food wasn't exactly gourmet and it wasn't very abundant. You would think after all the miracles they had seen and all the grace God had poured out on them, they would have at least an ounce of faith. No, all they could think of is that their bellies were not full.

It wasn't even that they were starving to death, they just didn't have everything they wanted, so they complained. They quickly forgot just how bad things were back in Egypt and how cruel Pharaoh was. They forgot how often they had been beaten, how much they and their children had suffered under Pharaoh's iron fist. How they were treated far worse than animals. Oh, none of this seemed to even enter their minds. Notice something though, God in His great love and wisdom, doesn't remind them, He does not simply say "Fine then go back to Egypt, since you think you had it so good". No, God in His great love and wisdom simply gives them nourishment. He gives them food straight from Heaven and they are happy and they rejoice and give God their thanks and adoration, for a short time. Think about it, if you or I were in God's place we surely would have lost patience with these self-centered, self-indulgent, ungrateful children rather quickly. We would probably have wiped them off the planet. We would have probably chosen to start fresh and do things differently. Thankfully, God sees things differently than we do. Think about it, we whine and complain all the time, God gives us answers, He gives us gifts and we don't even say thank you. It is a wonder that He still loves us so much.

How often do we do the exact same thing? God gets us out of a really bad situation and for a short time we're infinitely grateful. As time marches on we forget just how bad things really were. Daily pressures and demands start building up and we start grumbling and complaining. Then, to make it worse, we start reminiscing about the 'good ole days'. Just like the Israelites in the desert. We forget how bad things really were. At least it was familiar, comfortable, because it was all we ever knew, so what if things were really terrible, at least we knew what to expect, like getting beaten all the time, maybe it was some awful illness, or addiction. Whatever it was, we knew something had to change. Now we're in completely uncharted territory. Not knowing what is going to happen next, can be pretty darn scary. Now we start thinking about how things used to be. We seem to forget all the really bad parts. Maybe it was the 'good ole days' when you used to party all the time or the abusive relationship or well, you fill in the blanks there. You didn't have any responsibilities, you did what you wanted, when you wanted. Have you forgotten about waking up the next morning feeling horrible, disaster all around you, having to clean up the mess, being broke and/or broken? Maybe you don't realize that even if you don't have the perfect job and now you have bills to pay and responsibilities, now you also have a sense of self-worth and independence. Now you get to go places you never could in your party days and actually remember them. Now you know people who you value in your life and who truly value you. Now you have relationships that are meaningful. Now you have people in your life that you can trust. Now you have direction and are moving towards a future that means something to you.

We all have those times in our lives when we would rather go crawling back to a more comfortable place. We just have to remember how very far we have already come and be willing to face the struggles and hurdles life throws at us. We have to remember to put our faith and trust in God. In fact, it is the struggles and hurdles of life that strengthen us and add new depth to our existence. It is the experiences you have had to endure that will allow you to help someone else going thru the same things you have endured. Think about the person or people that have helped you and how much different your life is now, because God put them in your life.

Perhaps, you're having a hard time believing that God loves and cares for you. You really can't believe that anyone, let alone the God that created the entire universe really loves you and only wants what is best for you. You don't feel worthy. Maybe your only experience with love was anything but good and so you don't even know how to be truly loved the way it was meant to be.

You're right by the way, you, me, even Mother Teresa, are not and never can be good enough. That's the whole point. He loves us, and sent His Only Son to die a horrible death on the cross because our sins came with a huge price tag. One we could never afford to pay. We cannot earn His forgiveness; we cannot earn His love. He loved us first, He knew how completely lost we were and has a plan in place to bring us back to Him. If you are waiting till 'you're good enough', it will never happen. We don't do things to earn His love and acceptance. We accept the free gift of salvation and then through His love and kindness, mercy and grace, He begins to change us from the inside out. When we start realizing just how much God loves us, we start wanting to do things to please Him. We want to do things to honor Him and we want to show the world what a loving and merciful Father, He truly is. When you find something truly amazing you want to share it, you want everyone to know. Like when you go see a movie you really like or a great recipe or a new piece of equipment that works great and makes things easier or, well you get the idea. That thing, whatever it is, did not come into existence because of you, it already existed. When you discovered it, it made you happy for whatever reason and then you just had to go tell others about it. God has always existed, He is not something new that we created, something we just discovered. He has always been there. Like when America was discovered. Do you think that just because the boat was there that suddenly the North American Continent came into being, of course not. God's love for us does not happen because of anything we do. He loved us long before we even knew He existed. Things that His children do are not and should not be to try to earn His love. The things we do are in fact in response to the love He shows us. Sometimes it is really hard to comprehend such an awesome love, especially when you've never been shown true enduring love. God knows us, with all of our faults and flaws. He knows all of our weakness and mistakes. Every terrible thing we have ever done. He knew this even before we ever made our first mistake, before we had our first bad thought, before we were even born. God knew even then, just how bad we could be. With this knowledge, He put into place a wonderful plan to save us. A plan, to pay the enormous price for our sins, so that one day we could be with Him. Now that is an unfathomable love. That is just how much God loves you.

OUR OFFERINGS

We are commanded to give our tithes, but many people do not understand what that means. **"Bring ye all the tithes into the storehouse, that there be meat in Mine house, and prove Me now herewith, saith the Lord of hosts, if I will not open the windows of heaven and pour you out a blessing, that there shall not be room enough to receive it."** *Malachi 3:10 KJV.*

God wants us to be joyful givers, not to give just because, it is what we are told to do and because the Bible says so. Our giving is to be a joyful response to the love God has shown us. Many do not realize that we are not giving up something that is ours, but instead are simply giving back a small portion of what God has so graciously given to us. God uses what we give to continue to build His church, which by the way is not that building we gather in, it is the people that worship and believe in Jesus who died, and was resurrected to pay for our sins.

It is not up to us to decide where the money goes or how it is used. We don't even have to like what our church does with our tithe. All we have to do is give and trust God to use it for his purpose. He will use our tithes and offerings. I have yet to meet anyone who is powerful enough to change what God has planned, even a little bit. Sometimes it may appear that way for a time, but that's only because we can't see things from God's perspective. You know the Creator of the universe, the One who named all the stars in the heavens and numbered every hair on your head. When was the last time you managed any one of those things, so why do you think that He can't make sure that your tithes are used for his purposes? He has it all covered.

Offerings are separate from our tithes. Offerings are above and beyond our regular tithing. Say that maybe you have an unexpected windfall. You win the lottery, a rich uncle leaves you a lump sum of cash, or maybe you feel strongly that God is leading you to give a little extra. You can donate to specific causes above your regular tithe. Say a church building fund, an upcoming missions trip, maybe someone you know (in the church, maybe even someone who has never been to church is hurting and you want to help). What a wonderful way to show God's gracious love.

My husband and I have experienced that. One Sunday at church (we didn't go very often back then), the Pastor told the church that instead of putting donations in the offering plate, to bring it to whom they felt led. He had already asked those in need to stand. That was a hard thing for us to do and we had no idea what was going to happen. We had bills to pay and no way to pay them. Even now as I sit here typing this I'm tearing up at the thought of what happened next. People started getting up and walking over to those that had stood up. We got hugs and prayers and ended up with exactly enough money to pay our bills. No one there could have known what we needed and the money came from multiple people in different amounts. We weren't even regular attendees. God knew what we needed and lead others in the church to help us. To my recollection the handful of us that had stood that Sunday morning, all received exactly what was needed. Not all of it was financial. Some didn't need money, some needed the hugs, a shoulder to cry on, someone to let them know they were loved. This was the only time I've ever seen something like that done, but let me tell you it was an amazing experience. When we allow Him to, God can use us in some pretty amazing ways.

We have also been privileged to be on the giving end of that as well. I honestly can't tell you which was more of a blessing. Both were incredible, humbling experiences.

God wants to rain gifts down on us, but first, we have to be willing to follow the simple instructions that he gives us. This way he ensures that we are in fact ready to handle what he has for us.

If, for instance, we have the ability, to give a nice shiny new car to one of our children, would we give that new car to a five-year-old, hand him/her the keys and say "Have fun". First off the child would have no idea what to do with the keys, let alone the car. Even if the child figured out where the keys go and how to turn on the car with them, it would be dangerous to let that child go for, even a short drive. That is just common sense. Yet we whine and complain when God doesn't give us everything we want, right when we ask for it. Being the caring, loving Father that He is, He wants us to be prepared to receive and enjoy the gifts He has for us. He does not want us to go out and hurt ourselves or others because we just weren't ready for it yet. He watches us, gives us instructions and tests us first to make sure we are fully prepared for the gifts before He gives them to us. Then of course, if our arms are still full with what He has already given us, we have to be willing to set them down first, so that our arms are open and ready to receive more. In respects to tithing, He is not going to give us more financially, till we can handle what He has given us, in the first place and if we are not willing to do as He asks in giving back a small portion to help His church grow, then how can we expect to receive more. Who knows what we may decide to do with it. Of course, there are exceptions. Sometimes God gives us exactly what we ask for, because the only for us to learn, is to fall down a few times. You know, as for some of us hands on learners, we just have to jump in with both feet and get really messy. We as children, do not know nearly as much as we think. You know a lot of teenagers who believe they know everything, that's us. Certainly I must know far more than Daddy. We know everything, right. That's why we never make mistakes, never fail, and of course never ever hurt someone else's feelings. If only that were true. We, however, are all fallible human beings. God in all His great wisdom knows this and is extremely patient with us.

Over the years there are many things that I have asked for, especially concerning money, and God just didn't give me those things right then. Oh sure, my intentions were good, with thoughts of all the wonderful things that could be done with the money. Everything from donating money to help starving children overseas, to opening up a local youth center. Truly, if I had the money back then, even though my intentions were good, what would probably have happened is it would have been squandered on things that weren't needed before having the chance to use it the right way. Thinking about it, there would more than likely, would have been many wonderful experiences that would never have happened. So many things missed out on, amazing learning experiences He has given me over the years. I certainly would not have been where I am now.

By the way, things are far from perfect, but I have learned to appreciate things so much more and to worry so much less. That, at times, is far more difficult than you may imagine. As I sit working on this book, my husband and I are in a very difficult situation. We are flat broke, have broken pipes (the results of a very cold winter), so we have to shower at the neighbors (thank God for your wonderful neighbors), we run a hose through the kitchen window to do dishes. Our water pump works great, we just have broken pipes under the house, so we can't turn water on to the house and can't afford to get them fixed. Neither of us has a job, due to multiple health problems (me: bad back and knees, balance issues. My husband: cancer, heart problems and diabetes, just to name a few of his health issues), one house we're trying to sell, one we live in (no mortgage on either), lots of stuff we're trying to sell, and trying to plan another big move (we both strongly feel God wants us back out on the west coast). We can't get a loan because we're not working, can't get work because of health issues and bills are piling up. All and all though, I am very happy at this point in my life and wholly appreciate the blessings God has given me. This book, for instance, never in a million years would I have imagined I would want to write a book; let alone be able to. We have a roof over our heads, food in our bellies, three great kids and a wonderful church. We have learned, to trust that God knows what He is doing and what is best. Don't get me wrong, there are days when I have a great big old pity party, cry, whine, complaint and sometimes even yell at and argue with God. Then I realize, it is not all about me, this is God's work. You know what, He is a great listener and a great comforter, and very patient. He hasn't struck me down yet.

You may think, "Gee, you sound awfully dependent." You would be absolutely correct. We are made to be dependent upon the Father. We are after all His children. It makes much more sense to put my trust and faith in a God who knows all things and is perfect, then to put that trust and faith in myself. I make mistakes, lots of mistakes and definitely am not perfect. Perfection is something that though I may strive for, this side of Heaven will never attain. It is nice to know that the God of the universe, the Creator loves me, enough to watch over and guide me. Who in this world cares enough about you to allow you to mess up, even blame Him for all of your troubles and still be there for you? He is the only One who can truly 'make it all better'. **And God shall wipe away all tears from their eyes; and there shall be no more death, neither sorrow, nor crying, neither shall there be any more pain: for the former things are passed away. Revelation 21:4 <u>KJV</u>**. This is a promise, we as believers in Jesus have to look forward to and what a beautiful promise it is.

When we start to truly get that God has everything under control, loves us deeply and begin to truly trust in him, then and only then do we stop trying to "Save the Manna", simply because we know that God has always and will always take care of us and provide for all our needs. Every time I forget that God is Sovereign and really does have absolutely everything under control and has our best interest at heart, things start getting complicated, when trying to do it my way. That's when things really break loose. That's when God steps back and says "OK, go ahead and do things your own way. I'll be right here when you need me." He doesn't rub our noses in it when we mess up.

Think about how many times you have done things 'your way', only to realize later it would have been so much better if you had, in fact, listened to that 'still small voice'. God gently nudges you in the right direction. There we go again acting just like spoiled children, who know everything. You know like when we're told, don't touch the stove, it's hot. Well, of course, we reach right out and stick our hand on the stove. What do we do then, after burning ourselves? Then we step back and complain because we got burned and it hurt. Utter

71

shock and amazement, it was hot. First, we have to learn what 'hot' means. Guess what, often times we don't remember what happened and how much it hurt, or we think we're tougher now and have to prove it. Then, of course, we have to go try it all over again. Darned if we don't go stick our hand back on the hot burner again and get burned again. Wow, it hurt, just as bad this time as it did last time, maybe even more. It can be so hard to just let go and let God 'make it all better'. We are all just little children after all, and we just know that we can do it all by ourselves. Father, God steps back and lets us learn for ourselves. Sometimes He seems so very far away, but He is just giving us some space, however, He is never farther away than a simple prayer. All we have to do is to call out, reach for Him and He will run to us. He knows how to make it 'all better'. He is just waiting for us to truly call out to Him. He knows that if it is not from the heart, then we really don't mean it and will just turn and touch that proverbial 'hot stove", all over again. He knows that there are things that we just have to learn and experience for ourselves, in order to learn and grow, no matter how much it may hurt.

There are times when God may purposely expose you to things, to help you build up immunity to it. When my oldest son was just about 2-3 years old, the babysitter called early one morning to tell me that one of the children at daycare had the chicken pox and not to bring my son. We discussed it and the plan would stay the same, not because I wanted my son to suffer. By exposing him now, he would be able to get through it much easier than if he got the chicken pox as an adult and he would have the immunity so he would get it again later. Sure, he would go through some discomfort, but in fact, it would be the lesser of two evils, so to speak. In the same way, God will sometimes allow us to be exposed to things, and though we may have some discomfort, He knows that we will not have to suffer with it later because we will have built up immunity. What may cause discomfort now may cause great suffering or even death if we were not already resistant to it. God is truly magnificent. He loves us enough to do whatever is best for us, if even if we kick and scream and fight Him all the way.

If we could only see things through God's eyes, see things from His perspective, and then maybe we would stop throwing such terrible temper tantrums. Have you ever been around a child whose is having a temper tantrum? It's enough to drive anyone up the wall. Sometimes you'd do almost anything to, just make it stop. We are human and that is a very human response. We don't like beginning uncomfortable. Unfortunately, in the long run, it is the child that suffers when we give in. God, being a loving and just Father, knows how much damage could be done by giving in, just to make it stop. He knows that if we get our way, that we will not learn how to be strong, respectful and loving. We, in fact, will become self-centered and believe that everything revolves around us. We won't be able to stand strong and push forward when times get tough. Sometimes the best way to help someone is to expose them to the very things that, if faced later with no immunity, might permanently damage them.

Which is worse, to keep one sheltered so they never get hurt, never feel any discomfort or to let them feel no pain now and then, so they won't have to suffer tremendously for the rest of their lives, maybe even risk eternal death.

OK, there I go again down another rabbit trail. Where were we, oh yeah, tithes and offerings. My husband and I had an amazing friend and a wonderful man of God, who taught us a lot about how important tithing truly is. It is my belief, that if everyone were to tithe as we should, there would be much less, if any hunger in the world. Tithing isn't always about financial giving. Tithing is supposed to be the first and best of everything. I know, wow, that sounds even worse. Not just the first of your paycheck, which most of us don't do, but if you have a garden the first fruits of that garden and the best, a lumber mill the first and best of the lumber, your talents can and should also be given. You can and should give the first 10 percent (you get to keep the other 90 percent). Remember you are giving back to the King, the one who provided for your needs in the first place, so you should give your best. When someone gives so very generously don't you want to pay them back in kind? Isn't it only natural to want to do anything to pay them back, to thank them. Think about it, God does not need your money, your time or your talents. God already has everything. He wants us to give back, just a little to help grow His church, to show our faith and adoration in Him and to reap the incredible benefits of helping others.

My husband and I were blessed immensely when we got the opportunity to help with the new building our church was putting up. My husband, having been a painter for a number of years, offered to help paint the building and I then offered to help my husband. It was a wonderful experience. He was told that he could have bid on the job and gotten paid, but he felt strongly that this, in fact, was a way he could give back a little of what God had so graciously had given us.

Tithing can take many forms, not just financial. Oh, don't get me wrong, we tithed on our income as well. In fact, it tickled me so much being able to write those tithe checks that my prayers became, "God to help me give more". Wow, that's when things started really changing. Earnestly asking that God allow me to tithe more, my income started going steadily up and my tithe check got steadily bigger, bigger paychecks were an added bonus. Can't say that things will work the same for you. This is no magic formula, to make you rich. This is not prosperity gospel. I'm only saying that when we get our eyes off ourselves and start seeing things more from God's view it changes everything. Then, the church asked me to help with a couple different ministries over the next few months. Each time, they asked, it scared me, someone, anyone else could surely do a much better job. One of these would involve me, a female, going down to a men's homeless shelter to pick up bread, for our church. I had to think and pray about it for a while. When finally, and very reluctantly I said "Yes", it soon became clear what a wonderful blessing it was to bring bread to my church helping those in need, also getting to know some amazing men. Yes, they were down on their luck, had made some bad decisions, but for the most part, they were so determined to get their lives back on track. It was both an inspiration and an incredible blessing for me. God has a way of turning our sacrifices into wonderful blessings. In giving my time, I, in turn, was greatly blessed and will cherish that experience always.

Now imagine if all those who call themselves Christians tithed like they should. Financially giving just 10 percent (or more if you can and feel lead to), those with farms giving 10 percent of their produce (fruits, grains, vegetable, dairy, meat, etc). I honestly believe there would be no more hunger and no more need for welfare. Those with gifts such as construction, accounting, teaching and so on giving their talents to help others. Don't get me wrong, I'm not talking about free handouts, just saying that helping the poor, the needy, the sick, orphans and widows, etc., would make such a big difference in the world. That can and should include things like mentoring and teaching them how to be self-reliant and reach their potential. That is how the Bible tells us things should be. We spend so much of our time focused on ourselves, how amazing it would be to start focusing on help those around us instead. What a great way to show God unending love for us to the world.

LESSONS

God teaches us lessons even when we're not paying attention. Last night I was talking to a dear friend on the phone. She was going through some troubled times, I kept hearing things like, "I'm overwhelmed", "I'm depressed", "I don't know what to do". What do all those statements have in common? They're all 'I' statements. It's no wonder we are all so lost. We have either taken God completely out of the equation, or at least changed it enough so that the answer just won't come out the way we expect it to. Then we sit back and scratch our heads and wonder why two and two, no longer make four. If you take two plus two and change the plus sign to a minus, of course, the answer will not come out the same. Instead of four, you get a zero. Imagine that. You were still expecting the same answer, but now the equation is different and there for you get different results. So why is it, when we leave God out of our lives and things fall apart we're surprised. Now, instead of having the plus sign in the equation, there's a minus. That changes everything. Things just don't add up the way we expect them to.

We look around at the world today and see chaos everywhere. Instead of realizing that something is different or even missing in the equation, we play the blame game. Why does God, let such horrendous things happen? How can a loving and just God, let such bad things happen to good people? Why do, the innocent have to suffer? The questions go on and on. Not one of them is the right question. We fail to realize that we have changed the equation. It is not that God enjoys torturing us. In fact, as with any loving parent, it saddens Him greatly to see His children suffering, but He can't change all the rules to suit what we think is right at the moment. If He changes the rules, so that two minus two equals four, then that changes how all the numbers add up, or don't, as the case may be. Besides, being that He is a just God, He keeps all the rules the same all the time. That simplifies things for us. If we have always been taught that 2 plus 2 equals 4, then all of a sudden the rules change and 2 minus 2 equals 4, it's going to confuse a lot of people. Would that be fair or just? The whole world has to change for the sake of one. Then He would have to constantly be changing the rules, to fit this person or that person. Not to mention we would never learn anything, if every time we didn't like the way the numbers added up, He changed the rules to suit us. That truly would be chaos and cruel. We then could never know where we stand and what would happen next.

Have you ever had someone ask you to do something, and then change the rules? You did what they asked, the way they wanted it done, but know they are unhappy about it because they changed the rules and didn't even tell you. All that hard work for nothing. You may even have to start all over again. Guess what, you're almost done when they decide to change things up again. Maybe someone didn't like the way things were being done, so for that person, things were changed. You, again put forth your best effort, everything was going perfectly, then the rules changed. All your hard work and effort out the door, yet again. Now, how willing are you going to be to start all over again. Besides, this time, you know some others that the changes have hurt as well. What guarantee do you have that the rules won't get changed, again? Wouldn't that bother you and being confusing as well. Never quite sure what would happen next. When the rules would change. Who would be teacher's pet.

Imagine a pilot flying a plane, he's flying along just fine, when suddenly the weather turns bad. Now he can't even tell which way is up and which way is down. He gets disoriented and decides he better go a little higher just to be safe or to try to get above the clouds. What he fails to realize is that the plane is turned upside down and he ends up flying the plane into the ground. That may sound pretty bizarre, but I have heard of cases of that very thing happening. The rules didn't change; gravity didn't suddenly do a flip. No, the pilot became very disoriented and confused. The rules stayed the same, gravity still worked the way it always had. Up was still up and down was still down. Now if God stepped in and decided to change the rules for that one pilot, can you imagine the chaos it would cause for the rest of the world. If now up were down and down were up. God in His grace and wisdom does not change the rules, so the rest of the world continues as it was and most of the time nobody else even knows what happened. The incident is no less devastating, whether or not people on board live or die. It is still an awful thing. The rest of us continue on, if God had changed the rules for that one, then maybe the rest of us would have been killed. Do you see how that works? It is not that God hated or didn't care about the one, it's that He loves us all. We all have to deal with the consequences of our own actions, good and bad.

Not to mention that God doesn't change. He is the same yesterday, today and tomorrow. We can take comfort in that fact. We can easily know what to expect and what is expected of us. No guessing games. If you are not sure of the rules, then all you have to do is read the rule book. That's right, the Bible. It's all laid out in black and white. If you need a little help, you can go to your pastor, join a Bible study, you can even ask the Holy Spirit to help you understand. Kind of like having lifelines, and yes, you can phone a friend. Unlike in the game show, your lifelines are unlimited. You can and should open up your Bible, again and again, you should continue going the church and listening to the Holy Spirit. You really should continue praying for understanding and talking to God regularly. These are some of our 'lifelines'.

Imagine for a moment a little girl; let's say she's about four. She's beautiful, blonde hair, big blue eyes, and a smile that could melt even the coldest heart. Sure, she has the occasional temper tantrum, but what child doesn't? She brings great joy and light into your life, there is nothing you wouldn't do for this wonderful little girl. You go to visit her, but there is no one home. You try again and you call, but to no avail. Then you find out that her parents have taken her far away to a special hospital for children. You find out that she, in fact, has been diagnosed with an inoperable brain tumor. The temper tantrums were not normal childhood temper tantrums; they were in fact caused by her brain tumor. You can't go to her and the next time you see her is at her funeral, in her tiny little casket. I was about sixteen when I knew this beautiful little angel. How could a loving and just God allow such a beautiful little angel to suffer so? The part that most of us miss is how every many people, that little angel touched in her few short years. More people than most of the touch in our whole lifetime. We miss the fact that it brought her great joy to make others smile and laugh. We miss the fact the so many of the people whose lives she touched will be forever changed for the better by this child who was only here for a few short years. We don't know that if she had lived longer, that she may have suffered much more and that she may have forgotten how much God loves her. This little angel personally touched my life and brought me great joy. I know just how deeply she touched my life in those few short months. Sitting here with tears in my eyes, remembering how much I miss her, someday we will again get to see each other. Oh, what great joy she brought me. Heaven only knows how many others will be lined up to thank her as well. What an incredible gift she was to all of us that knew her. Though the loss of her is great, I am forever changed and thankful that God took her home with Him. She will never again know pain and suffering.

Now imagine an old lady, alone trapped in her own house by her failing health. This woman has endured a lifetime of abuse (both physical and emotional), this woman has survived the great depression and is afraid of the world because of all she has endured. She is also strong and loving, kind and caring. Why, because this woman knows God personally and deeply loves Him. This also was someone I personally knew. She was one of the signally most influential people in my life. She was a great woman of faith, radiated Gods love so brightly. It was hard not to be warmed by her presence. This wonderful lady had more reasons to complain and be angry than most anyone I have ever met. This woman showed me the power of God's great love. She showed me the healing power of His mercy and grace. I know that if she had not experienced the things she did; she would not have been the great lady she was. She was not famous; you will not find her in any history book. The one book that her name is in, is the Lambs Book of Life. Towards the end her mind was going, she thought her very abusive, ex-husband had come back to try to kill her and in her mind, Armageddon was actually happening. This woman's faith never wavered, she never doubted God, even with everything she believed was happening. Through her, I came to know God better and I am forever thankful for her presence in my life. Someday we will be, "dancing on the streets of gold", together. Her mother, whom she spoke of often, and the angel's heaven will be there rejoicing with us.

If we were truly able to see things through God's eyes, just maybe we would be able to see that there is far more beauty in this world than we could possibly imagine. I thank God, for the amazing people he has put in my life and the very many ways they have touched me and shaped who I am. I thank God, for what most people would consider terrible things that have happened to me. Without these people and things in my path, to help guide me, I would not be who and where I am today. Maybe instead of blaming God for everything that is wrong in the world, we should be thanking Him for using even the bad things to help us and guide us. Only with God can one sinful person plus one incredible Savior equal one redeemed child of God. Oh, how blessed we truly are.

The best part of all these tests God gives us is that not only are they 'Open Book' tests, we can open up our Bible anytime we need to. If we have a hard time finding the answers all we have to do is ask and the Teacher will tell us where to find the right answer and if that is not enough, He will gladly give us our own private tutor, the Holy Spirit, to help us with the answers. That's not to say it is an easy test. We would not learn much if it were too easy. We learn and grow the most, through difficult times and circumstances. Of course, we as children already know all the answers. Just like most children we think we have everything figured out, we know far more than Daddy. We haven't even figured out the basics. We know what we know, of course, we just know that we're right. Then, when we are proven wrong, we dig in our heels that much more and insist that we just have to be right. Fortunately, since we don't fail the tests, we have as many chances as we need to get it right and all the help we could ever need. That, however, is one of the biggest parts of the problem, since we already feel we have all the right answers, why would we ever need any help? You know that surely the teacher must be picking on you, or maybe He changed the rules just because He wants to see you fail. If we admit that we are wrong, everybody will think we're stupid and laugh at us.

I was at an Amway convention a number of years back and heard this wonderful little lady up on stage, saying that Gods give us tests, but unlike in school, we can't fail them. He just keeps giving them to us till we get it right. That was a huge slap in the face for me. I remember thinking God help me get the test right the first time, I hate taking tests over and over again. I would much rather move on to something new. Remember after all, this is an open book test. Take out your book, The Bible and open it up. Your tutor is the Holy Spirit; He is always there to help you. Just ask Him to explain it, to help you to understand. He will and in some pretty amazing ways. He knows how you learn and there for knows how best to explain things in your terms, so you can 'get it'. First, however, you have to be willing to ask for His help and then actually listen to what He is telling you. That may mean you have to admit that you don't know all the answers already.

Why is it that we have the audacity to think should know all the answers? Why do we presume to think, that we're smarter than the greatest Teacher ever, the One who truly does have all the answers? We're human; we're mortal and very much fallible, no matter how brilliant we think we are. However, we puff up and strut around like a peacock trying to make the whole world think we're so great. Don't get me wrong, God obviously does not make junk, however, we are also not perfect. Jesus, even though He was perfect Himself, always referred back to the Father God and the written word of God.

So if Father, Son and Holy Spirit are all separate yet one, how could Jesus not know all the answers? My thought on that is, Jesus was in human form. Like us a mortal being at the time and as a mortal there were certain things that the Father God restricted from him. If He, while here with us on earth, walking as a man, knew all things as His Father God in heaven did, then why would he cry out to Father God in the garden, ***"Oh my Father, if it be possible, let this cup pass from me: nevertheless not as I will, but as thou wilt." Matthew 26:39 KJV.*** Jesus knew that His Father's will was and is perfect. He knew how deeply God Loves Him and us. Jesus knew in His great torment and anguish that His Father in heaven knew what was best and had all the answers and that for the great love He had for us, His sacrifice alone would save us, His beloved children.

As human beings and mortals if we were to have all the answers and truly know what is ahead of us, for one we in our infinite wisdom would undoubtedly try to change things. We are not perfect. Can you imagine billions of people all wanting things their own way, because each of us just knows we're right? The chaos would be unimaginable. God in his great wisdom, only allows us to know so much, so that we will learn to trust in Him. So that we will go to

Him for the answers and so we will open up a dialog and build a relationship with Him. You see, God is not power hungry. He does not have to be; He already has all the power. He does, however, very much want a meaningful relationship with His beloved children. In case you weren't sure, that means us, you and me.

When you truly and completely love someone, you can tell them anything and everything. You entrust them with your deepest, darkest secrets. You want them involved in your whole life. You tell them about your hopes and dreams, about things that excite you and things that make you happy, things that make you laugh, things that make you cry, even things that make you angry. Being that they are such an important part of your life you want them with to share in the good and the bad. Their opinions are important to you. You ask them for help when you can't find your car keys and when you need advice on how to handle some frustrating situation. If we are so willing to go to our parents, our spouse, our best friend, even the next door neighbor, why is it that we try to hide so much of ourselves from our Creator, our Father, the One who calls us friend. He wants to know us intimately; He wants to be part of every aspect of our lives. Oh, by the way, He knows where you put your keys, ask Him, you might be amazed at how differently things go when you have God in every aspect of your life. Talking with God is not just for some priest or a religious guy sitting in the church pew. The fact is God wants us, as we are, battered and broken. We can't really do much to change ourselves, we can only be willing to let God change us. When we have finally surrendered, He will make something beautiful out of your broken pieces. God loves you and wants to call you friend.

If we go to God with all of our flaws and brokenness and sincerely ask Him to help us, then He can make us into something truly beautiful. We are His beloved children and He deeply cares about and for us. That is also why He does not and will not force His will on us. He wants a deep, intimate relationship with us. He doesn't want a bunch of mindless robots running around. He doesn't need a bunch of simple servants. He doesn't expect us to be perfect when we come to Him. That's His job, to perfect us. We are after all a bunch of cracked pots, we are broken, shattered, let's face it we are a mess. It is only when we realize this, that we are not able to fix ourselves, we'll finally understand the only way to fix our brokenness is to go to the Master Craftsman; broken and messy as we are. He can not only put us back together; He can make us into something magnificent. He can make us better than we ever thought we could be.

WAGING WAR

Sometimes the only way you can become the best you, that you can be, is to be totally and completely broken. The military figured that one out a long time ago.

The first week of training, when you go into the military is a process of breaking you down, so that they can build you back up into something better, stronger and more able to work well on a team. This ability to work with the team and react to situations could someday save your life, when you find yourself in a war situation. You go into the military with all your years of experience, your preconceived ideas of how things are. You, in your mind, have everything figured out. You're going to be the best soldier ever and surely won't need hardly any training, because you already "know it all". Heck they might just as well make you a four star general and put you in charge of everything, because you know you're just that good.

So it begins. The military knows that until they break all of those preconceived ideas you have of just how great you are; they will not be able to build you up to be the best that you can be. The very first week of training, they push you as hard as they can. They treat you like dirt. They run you ragged. They are going to do whatever it takes to break you down.

I remember my oldest son calling home during that first week of training. He sounded so completely broken. As a mother, that was one of the hardest phone calls ever. He wanted me to come get him. He just couldn't take it. He wasn't good enough, he wasn't strong enough, he wasn't smart enough. He just wasn't military material. As a mother, everything inside me was screaming at me to hop in the car and drive as fast as I could go and get him. It broke my heart and yes, it was hard holding back the tears. My son, six foot four inches tall, big, strong, smart, ambitious and a heart of gold, crying on the phone, asking me to come and bring him home. Realizing at that moment what was going on, desperately wanting to go get him, instead, I told him to stick it out, that he could do it. It was hard holding back the tears till the phone call was over. The next time he called, about a week later, he sounded like a completely different person. He sounded more confident, stronger, more secure. He still had a lot of training to go through, but now he could be trained. They had broken him down so that they could build him up to be the best he could be.

Sometimes God does something like that with us. He knows that the only way we can get over ourselves, is to let us become broken. It is when we are truly broken that we realize just how little we know and just how much we need our Father God. It is then, that we understand that we just can't do it all ourselves, that we don't 'know it all'. That we need someone to clean up the mess we have made of things and fix our broken pieces. It is at that point that God can start His glorious work in us and begin making us into something truly amazing. It is then that we start seeing things from a whole new perspective. It is in those, shattered moments, that we begin to realize just how much God truly loves us. He has stood by allowing us to make our own mistakes, as heartbreaking as it is for Him. He has waited patiently for us to call out to Him for help and runs to us with open and loving arms to embrace us and welcome us home. Just as in the story in the Bible about the **prodigal son.** If you're not familiar with it, you can find it in ***Luke15:11***. In that story after the younger son had taken his inheritance and squandered it on prostitutes and wild parties, he decides to go back home and offer himself as a servant to his father. Even the servants had more than enough to eat and a warm place to sleep. Since he had blown through all of his inheritance and the place where he was living was having a major famine, his life had gotten pretty darn messy. Even what he was feeding the pigs was looking pretty tempting. When he returns home, his father runs to him, throws his arms around him and tells the servants to prepare a party for his son. Only the best of the best will do, for his son has returned home to him. In this way, God pours out His amazing grace on us and ever so gently picks us up and dusts us off and begins putting us back together. It is in our brokenness that we are finally able to lose our arrogance.

Now He can begin a great work in us. Ever so carefully putting us back together. Making us "better, stronger, faster". If we started out this way with all our self-worth and arrogance, we would probably do an enormous amount of damage to ourselves and others before we understood what a loving and gracious God we have. This is why He allows us to learn for ourselves and come to Him when we are ready. Though He is always nearby, keeping a watchful eye on us, always close enough to hear us when we finally decide to cry out to Him.

Unlike in the military you won't have some drill sergeant in your face telling you're a worthless dirtbag, well not from God's side of things. The devil is however really good at pointing out and magnifying every little flaw. We are, of course, really good at beating ourselves up, we really don't need much help in that department. God just allows us to make our own decisions and our own mistakes. When we finally come to the end of ourselves and realize that the universe does not revolve only around us, then God can step in and pick us up and start putting us back together the way He meant us to be. We, in the hands of the Master Craftsman can become something magnificent. This doesn't happen overnight, for most of us. God can do anything, of course, He knows what will not only be best for us, but also for those whose lives we will touch. Sometimes others need to see the transformation and sometimes so do we, in order to believe it's real. Sometimes those whose lives we will touch need to see and know that God loves us know matter what. That even a messed person like us can be changed. If He can love and can fix us in all of our brokenness, then just maybe He can and will love and fix them too.

God as a good and just Commander and Chief, our fearless leader, knows the battles ahead of us and wants us to be well prepared to deal with what the enemy will throw at us. He wants to equip us with the right weapons and outfit us with the right uniforms, the whole Armor of God, ***Ephesians 6:10-18***. To be well prepared takes training and training doesn't happen overnight. You wouldn't take a brand new recruit and throw him on the front lines with the enemy marching with guns blazing. Of course not, the new recruit would be a 'sitting duck', he wouldn't stand a chance. You first need to learn to, not only to trust your commanding officer, you need to learn good teamwork and good tactics, what weapon to take into battle and how to use them.

We are not in this alone. God already sent in His own best for you, Jesus. Jesus came into the full blown battle, the enemy waging war on us. We were already captured and being held in the enemy's camp, enslaved, being beaten and tortured. He already knew there would be a great ransom to pay. Jesus knowing this willingly laid down His weapons and marched headlong into the enemy's camp and traded His Own Life for that of ours. Trading Himself for us, those who did not even know of Him. Those who would be ungrateful for His amazing sacrifice. Allowing the enemy to instead beat and torture Him. The One who had done absolutely nothing wrong, taking our punishment and paying our debt, ending the battle. This does not mean we will not still face battles, but Jesus ended the war. What the enemy didn't know, is that Jesus had a secret weapon in this war for our souls. Jesus in laying down His life and then being resurrected, had bought our salvation through grace, the greatest weapon of all against the enemy. One for which the enemy has no defense, except to try and make us believe it isn't real or that we really don't need it.

God is there leading the charge and has teamed us up with other soldiers, some are battle worn veterans and some are new recruits. I don't know which you are, but I do know we all need Jesus, our commander and chief to lead the charge, to show us the right battle plan and how best to attack the enemy's camp. He, God has set up the best training possible, so that you will be prepared for what the enemy will throw at you. Other Christians are so important to our own spiritual well-being; we need them for the spiritual warfare we will be doing. Make no mistake about it, we are in an all-out war, not just for ourselves, but also for the souls of the rest of God's children. It is, for the most part, an invisible battle. Our fight is in the spiritual realm. The devil has every intention of causing us to run, straight into the pit of hell. Our weapons are not guns and knives. Our weapons are God's truth, His word, faith and of course prayer. Prayer is like a laser guided smart bomb, on steroids. There was a movie that came out recently where an elderly lady explains to her granddaughter about her, 'war room'. It is not a room with maps and computers with satellite links, no her 'war room' is a room that she goes into, to pray. A place set aside where she goes away from the distractions of the world, where she can focus on the battle that all Christians face, the battle between good and evil.

This is a battle for the souls of men, women and children. With our prayers, we petition God for other people, for our schools, for our politicians, and for whatever else God lays on our hearts to pray for. It may be for a specific person and/or need, or it could be for something less specific. Our prayers, whatever they are for, they are none the less our most powerful weapons against the enemy. Only too often we do not put very much weight on praying. That is exactly what the devil wants. He does not want us to realize what a powerful weapon our prayers are. It's like having that smart bomb, a targeted and deadly accurate, that can go in and take out the enemy, leaving no collateral damage. He (satan), does not want us to realize just how effective our prayers are. Even science a few years back said that not only does prayer work, but that the person does not even need to know they are being prayed for. If we could see into the spiritual realm when we pray, we would see our prayer going out and lighting up the sky. We would see them slamming into and crushing the enemy's camps. We would see the great battle we are waging in all its fury and how we are in fact defeating the enemy and destroying his strongholds. The only way for satan to defeat our prayers is to make us believe that they don't matter and that our prayers are having no effect. Don't believe that for one second. As long as our prayers are in line with God's will and not just empty and selfish, they have great power. If you want to nuke the enemy's camp, obliterate his forces, then maybe it's time that we get on our knees and together with other believers in a prayer group, you know like calling in the special forces, and start demolishing the enemy's camps. When we join forces with other believers, we become a force to be reckoned with. There is not only safety, but also great strength in numbers. This by no means makes your single prayers less powerful or less important. Do not believe the enemies propaganda, that tells us that prayer doesn't work or that it has little if any power, prayer is our most powerful weapon.

This brings me to our next great and powerful weapon, the word of God, the holy Bible. If prayer is our most powerful weapon, say like a cannon, then we have to have the gun power and cannon balls to load it with. By reading and knowing the Bible, we are equipping ourselves, both with knowledge on how to use that cannon and the ammunition to load it with. Have you ever seen a cannon sitting in front of a military base or at a park? They can be pretty tough looking. Ultimately, they are just a big hunk of metal. You need to know how to use them and then have the right ammunition to load them with before they will do much good. Oh and don't forget even with all of that if you forget to light the fuse it still won't do anything. With the right instructions and ammo, they can be a deadly weapon. That is why we need the right instruction manual and ammo, that would be the Bible.

By reading His word we grow to understand God and what He wants for His children. It teaches us about every aspect of life. We most certainly need help understanding it. There is, after all a lot of information in it. This is why it is so important to surround ourselves with God's children. In this way we not only learn from them, we also help them learn as well. We help keep each other on the straight and narrow, so we don't get led down some rabbit hole and lost in a proverbial wonderland like Alice. That, after all, can be a very scary place. You really don't want to end up in the middle of enemy territory without backup and with no way out. Back to prayer, it is also the hotline, directing to God. Use it and He will send in the reinforcements you need.

This is why the church is so infinitely important to us as believers. We need the church, which is in fact other Christians not the brick and mortar. We are the body of the church and a body has many parts. No one part more important than the next. We must all work together to function properly. The body minus one ear can still hear, but will miss out on some sounds on that deaf side. The body minus an arm can still function, but has to learn to adjust, how to get things done. The body can function with only one kidney and no one else may ever know, but you still have to make certain adjustments. I think you get the picture. We can function without all the parts, but that's not how we were meant to work. Things just go more smoothly when we all work together.

We may very well end up in a few battles before we are completely trained and some things you just have to learn through experience. Our general, our leader, well He's right there with us leading the charge. He knows the enemy's strengths and weaknesses, He has mapped out the territory and has a battle plan in place, we just need to listen to His instructions and follow his lead. Don't forget your battle armor and weapons. You know the helmet of salvation, the breastplate of righteousness, the belt of truth, the shield of faith, the sandals of peace and the sword of the spirit. ***Ephesians 6:10-18N (NIV).***

It is when we go off on our own, half-cocked and unprepared, that we end up in a lot of trouble. It is then when we seem to have no way out, trapped in enemy territory, that we need to call out to God for help. We need to accept His wonderful gift of salvation through the sacrifice Jesus made us. Call out to God and He will gladly send in His special forces to pull you out of the enemy's camp.

PRAYER: TALKING TO DADDY

Personally, I talk to God all the time. When I wake up in the morning, driving somewhere in my car, in the kitchen cooking and when falling asleep at night. Nothing is too small to talk with Him about, silly things, deep concerns, ask Him for advice and sometimes when really mad and/or frustrated, my end of the conversation may at times get a bit loud. That's right at times, there's yelling and complaining involved. Then when I'm done having my temper tantrum, I ask God for help. God patiently listens, He comforts me. Then it's time for me to, sit back and listen.

I truly want to hear what God wants to tell me. I am never disappointed. He is a very patient and wise King and He loves me very much, that goes for you too. God deeply loves all of His children. God made each of us unique and special. I know also that He loves you deeply. God does not play favorites. He loves us all equally and equally wants the same deep relationship with you. He will, however, talk to us differently and listen to us differently. We are after all each unique individuals, He made us that way. Never think that something that is important to you is not important enough to tell God. He, like any good parent wants to know the details of what's happening in your life. The good things, the bad things, the things that make you angry and even the silly little things that make you giggle.

If all that talking seems a bit much to you, then start with a few minutes a day. Something as simple as "Hey God, thank you for this day and help me do well today." how about "Good morning God", or "Jesus, thank you for all you did for me." The point isn't to say some big, fancy prayer. The point isn't to get all the words right. The point is to start talking with God. The more you talk with Him, the more comfortable you will get talking with Him and the more you will want to talk with Him. God doesn't want some religious person sitting in a pew, reciting some scripted words, He wants us to talk with Him from our heart. After all, that basically is all that prayer is, talking with God. Really talk with Him, like you would a close friend. He wants to build a deep and lasting relationship with you. Yes, as I spoke of recently, prayer is also our most important weapon. We must never forget that. In order to petition God on behalf of the situation and other people effectively, we need to we need to build a relationship with the One we are praying to. The better we know our Creator, the easier it will be to know how and what to ask Him for help with. You will be able to come to Him more boldly and with more confidence to petition for people and things we need Him to help with. Don't forget how important reading the Bible is. The Bible, after all, is God's word and what better way to get to know Him than by reading what He has said. The more you know about God, the deeper the conversations, your prayers, will be with Him.

Did you by chance notice how often the word 'with' is being used?

When you talk 'with' someone you're having a conversation, a dialogue, it's two sided. When you talk to someone, it's a monologue, you're doing all the talking and many times even if the other person wanted to say something they can't get a word in edgewise. We need two-sided conversations. Not just endless ramblings and meaningless words. Conversations build relationships. Remember what God ultimately wants is a real relationship with you. He wants to know about the big things and the little things. He wants you to tell Him about what makes you laugh and what makes you cry. God always has the time for you, especially when you speak with Him from your heart. When you cry out from the depth of your soul and in your brokenness lay everything down before him that is when things, really start to happen. When you call out to God and come before him with open arms and empty hands. When we truly admit how very broken we are and ask God to fix us, to make us into what He intended us to be. That is when God can pour out the great abundance He has for you, because it is then that you are no longer loaded down, it is then that you begin to understand that it is only God's great and abundant grace and love that can fill the void that you for so long had tried to fill with things.

THE HAMSTER CAGE

Have you been trying to fill this enormous void with all the things the world tells you will make you whole, make you powerful, and make you loved, make you important? When after a lifetime of feeling that void becoming deeper and wider and nothing is even making the slightest dent in it, you know there is something more, something to fill that deep hole in your heart. In fact, the hole keeps getting bigger and bigger. The world tells you that you need to make more money, be more beautiful, be smarter, and try harder, do more, own more toys.

Those things the world tells you will make you happy, will only deepen the hole and widen the gap. You feel like a hamster on a wheel, in a cage. You keep running faster and faster, but you're not getting anywhere. The fact is, you're just getting more tired and more frustrated. Even when you finally decide to jump down off that infernal wheel and stop running for nothing, you find yourself trapped inside your little hamster cage. You can see outside the cage, but only just outside the cage and you cannot imagine there could be much more than what you can see. Maybe you figure what is the use; you have given up and decided to just exist inside your little cage. You may, however, have seen a glimpse of something beyond this little space in which you exist and just maybe there is more out there, maybe the rumors you have heard about something much bigger than you, are true. Oh, but maybe that much bigger thing will come and crush you. How could something that big possibly care about you. Surely you are not important enough for this Great Giant to have the time for you, and anyway, surely it is only a myth after all. Have you come to the end of yourself yet? Are you ready to take the chance and cry out from inside your little cage or will you just continue to exist there? Hop back up on that wheel. Maybe if you run fast enough, you'll get somewhere, find what you're looking for. After all, isn't that what all the other good little hamsters are doing?

When you finally, for whatever reason decide to call out, in comes this Great Giant. You shake and maybe even try to hide. In spite of your great fear and doubt, something inside of you tells you just surrender and call out and trust (have faith). As the Great Giant reaches down inside your little cage and lifts you up, you know He will not hurt you. He is there to help and protect you. He is there to love and nurture you. As you are lifted up, not only out of your cage, but above all those things just outside your cage, you can start to see how much more you were missing out on. You start to see things more clearly. Then new and wonderful things come into focus. How small was that little cage you were in and how different things look from outside that cage. You can begin to feel the warmth of God's immense love for you and finally get a glimpse of the wonders that God has had in store for you all along. You begin to realize that you are not just a little hamster, destined to be trapped in a cage and running on wheel, the rest of your life. You start to realize that you are in fact important, not because of who you are, but because God the Father loves you. From here, if you look back at where you were, you start to realize just how confined you were. Do you know who put you in that little cage and kept you so afraid of the Great Giant that was outside? That's right the devil, satan, the great deceiver. As long as you're so wrapped up in your little cage and/or too afraid of the Great Giant (God), outside, you'll never call out, you will never be saved. Of course, the last thing the devil wants is for you to be saved and realize that you are in fact a beloved child of God, you are very important to Him, not just a hamster in a cage and that He has great and wonderful things in store for you. You're really not that caged little hamster after all. You are a beloved child of God.

God created you to be glorious. He has incredible things in store for you. God, however, will not force His will on you. You have every right to stay snugly in your little cage, running on your little wheel. You were created with a free will, so He waits patiently for you to call out to Him. He is ready to come take you out of your cage and show you what true freedom is, outside the cage.

He waits patiently for you to call out to Him so that He may not only show you the wonders that you have been missing out on, He also wants to lavish His great love on you.

When you come to God, the whole of Heaven celebrates. There is great rejoicing that you, like the 'prodigal son' of the Bible, have returned home. You are, that important to Father God. He loves you that much. You know there is actually a whole other part of that story that we don't even think about. My Pastor recently talked about the other son in a sermon. In that story, Jesus started out by saying, **"A certain man had two sons."** *Luke 15:11 KJV.* We hear a lot about the son who gets his inheritance and goes out to a far land and squanders it and then comes home to his father. Now think about the other son, the one who stayed home and worked for his father, you might assume that he is the good son. Surely he must be better than the other son. He did not ask for his inheritance early, (Meaning dear old dad had to liquidate at least part of the estate to give his one son the cash he was demanding, what a slap in the face. "Hey dad, I don't really care about you, just give me my money so I can go party.") The father does just that. It's not that he didn't care, he had already done everything he could to raise this son right, now he would have to learn for himself.

Anyway, back to the other son. You know the one that stayed home, the one we all assume was the good son. We do at least know this other son was the older son. We also know if we read on, after he finds out that dear old dad is throwing a party because his younger brother has returned, **"And he was angry and would not go in; therefore, came his father out and entreated him."** *Luke 15:28 KJV.* Now you would think that he would be happy that his little brother had returned, but no, he was so angry that he would not even

104

go inside and join the celebration, his father actually had to leave the party and his guests and go out and beg the older son to come in. Not quite the good son we thought he was. To further add insult to injury the older son goes on to complain how hard he worked since little bro took off. He goes on to complain, **"Lo, these many years do I serve thee, neither transgressed I at any time thy commandment: and yet thou never gavest me a kid (young goat), that I might make merry with my friends."** *Luke 15:29 KJV.* Can you feel the love and respect? Dad has provided everything this son needed and yet he appears to despise his loving father. I've worked hard for you, not thanks for giving me a job. Oh, and by the way I wanted to have a party with my friends and you didn't supply the food, gee must I pay for my own supplies for my party? Do you see the problem here? We can assume he is an adult child, but does not wish to act like an adult, so everything must be dad's fault. He has a nice house to live in (dad is a wealthy man), plenty of food and servants. Sure, he is probably expected to work, at the family business since he is an adult. Did you catch this son's claim of being all but perfect? I've kept all your commandments and worked for you all these years. I would imagine he has messed up at least a few times. Now little brothers back and instead of being happy, he gets mad at his loving father for showing the younger brother love, kindness and mercy. Wow, talk about a self-centered son. He's an adult son living at home with everything provided for him, but everything he feels is wrong is all dear old dad's fault. Of course, we never, ever blame anyone else for what we think is wrong is our lives.

Well, now, let's get back to the hamster cage. God,in fact, doesn't just sit ideally by watching us run endlessly on that wheel. It gives Him no great delight seeing you trapped in your little cage. You are far too important to Him too for that. He has been calling out to you. He has been bringing you fresh water and food. He has been feeding you, just like the Israelites wandering in the desert. He knows that from inside your little cage you can't get fresh food and water for yourself. He wants you to be well fed, so when you finally allow Him to take you from your cage, you will be alive and well. If He did not feed you, you surely would become malnourished and die. Even when we are too wrapped up in our own little world to think about God or even realize He is there, God is infinitely aware of us. He actively waits, protecting us from unseen evils that would come to destroy us. He sends us the Holy Spirit to keep us company and help guide us down off that infernal wheel.

God cannot live inside that cage. Let's face He's just too big. He can see us in there. He knows what's happening inside our little cage. Sometimes that is part of it, God is just too big for us to see. We mistake Him for something else. He most surely cannot be real. Not something so much bigger than we are. Not something that knows every inch of our little hamster cage. After all this cage is our whole world, there can't possibly be anything outside of it. How foolish to think that there can possibly be more to life than what we know is the entire world, our entire reality. If there is, it is too big and too scary to think about. Better to just ignore it and stay safe right where we are.

Isn't it about time to call out and ask God to take us out of the hamster cage, away from the infernal wheel, we have spent so much time running on to get nowhere fast. Isn't it time to realize we were never meant to be hamsters in a cage and that the Father has much more and better things in store for you. We just have to be willing to let Him lift us out of the hamster cage we have kept ourselves locked in for so long. Oh dear God, please get me off this infernal wheel so I can actually go somewhere and accomplish what you have for me.

IN THE DESERT

Sometimes it is only through our isolation, through our time spent alone in a vast desert, that we are finally able to see God. Through these times of quiet solitude, when all of the noise of the world is so far away, that we are finally able to hear the voice of God. True, that in these times we can most certainly, more clearly hear the devil telling us how worthless we are and how horrific our circumstances are, but without all the other sounds clamoring in the background, we are finally able to hear God speaking to us. When we get the mountains of pride and self-doubt out of the way, it is much easier to see what has been right in front of us all along. Now, we can see the Father's loving arms stretched out waiting to embrace us. Now, we can see His loving smile shining on our lives and we can in our brokenness accept what He has been so freely offering to us all along, His love and mercy.

What is a desert? Deserts are the times when everything seems to have fallen apart, when our lives seem to have fallen into total chaos, when we reach the end of ourselves and only have one way to turn, to God. When *our* plans have utterly fallen apart and there is absolutely no way for us to put the pieces back together. When we are utterly lost. In these times, there are only so many choices we can make. Oh yes, we still have choices, we still have free will. God has graciously taken away most of the excess and narrowed the choices down for us and a lot of the time He has a big neon arrow pointing us to the right answer in the middle of our dark, empty desert. Now the path is slowly coming into view. The path He has laid out for us.

Only too often, even in the middle of the desert, we miss the point. Remember, God's children wandered around in their desert for 40 years. Do you think maybe, they missed that big neon sign? Think about it, God's chosen people had Him there with them. **"And the Lord went before them by day in a pillar of a cloud, to lead them the way; and by night in a pillar of fire, to give them light; to go by day and night"**. ***EXODUS 13:21 KJV.*** That sounds a lot like a great big neon sign to me. Yes, God, let them choose to disobey Him. There is that free will thing, again.

We are constantly trying to put the blame on God for the results of the decisions we ourselves have made. We expect our Father to just make it all better. The problem with that is, we would never learn anything. God knows this and wants us to grow and learn. He lets us make our decisions and deal with the consequences. This way we may learn and not have to keep making the same painful mistakes over and over again.

Have you ever been in a desert? It can be an unforgiving place, extreme heat in the daytime and extreme cold at night, miles and miles of nothing but sand. It may be days; months or even years in between rains. The things that live there are very tough. They have to be in order to survive there. The desert is a desolate, dry place, with very little signs of life. Oh, but when the rains do come and drench the perched ground, suddenly everything springs to life. The seeds that have for so long lain dormant in the ground, begin to grow and produce such beauty. Living creatures come out of there shelter and wonderfully, this once barren, desolate place is thriving with life and full of great beauty.

God wants to bring life and beauty into your dry parched existence, but first, you may need to go through a time of great drought. To top that off, the storm that comes to bring life back into your desert may appear unbelievable and very scary. The winds will blow, torrents of rain will fall and surely you will get either be swept away or pummeled into the ground. God, who just happens to be the original Master Gardener, knows what it will take for your garden to grow and flourish. Did you know that there are actually seeds that will not grow till they have been through a fire? He can make some things amazing, even out of something that seems completely horrible.

Anyway, back to our desert. Where were we? Oh, that's right, we are in the middle of our vast dry desert. On the horizon, we can see the storm clouds building, the clouds getting darker, winds are picking up, lightning flashes brightly and you can hear the thunder rumble across the desert floor. If you're like me you might be a bit apprehensive, since you have no shelter, but essentially storms excite me. I can feel the energy, intensifying. If you ever see some crazy person out dancing in an all-out storm, it may just be me. I know that the storm will bring renewed life and wash away the dirt and grime that have built up. However, a large number of people are very much afraid of storms. Afraid of the loud crashing thunder, afraid of the howling winds, the lightening crashing down around them, the rain washing them away. Whether it's because of having been through a storm that ripped through your life and changed everything; or maybe because of those scary movies that so many like to watch or just because you are. The fact is that storms will come, like it or not, without those storms the desert places in our lives will remain dry and barren, without color and unable to spring forth life. Storms bring the winds of change, to blow away the things that are keeping us from growing and the drenching rains to wash away the dirt and grime and nourish and restore us. Did you know that plants will actually grow better and stronger after an all-out storm than from irrigation? I have seen this, we live in farm land U.S.A., corn fields all around. I am always amazed at how much better the crops grow after a thunderstorm. During the storm things can seem pretty scary, but when you come through the storm and look out across the landscape of your life, you may just see how God has brought forth beauty from what was once a barren wasteland. Where once there was nothing, an empty unforgiving endless desert and miles of sand, now there is something beautiful and thriving.

Rejoice, oh my children that the storm is coming. Fear not the change the storm will bring to the landscape of your life. I have only good things in store for you. The storms come to wash away all the grim that the world has piled up on you, and to quench you and revive and renew you. I shall bring forth great beauty out of the desert times of your life, through the raging storms.

When things seem to be at their absolute worst, that is usually when you can expect your biggest breakthrough. When you see life's storm clouds building on the horizon and can see the lightening flashing in the distance and hear the thunder rumbling, that may seem like the scariest place to be. You know it's coming; you can feel the winds of change. Change can be very scary. When it's all over, even though you may have to pick up the pieces and start all over again, it's a fresh new start and if you will just ask, admit you need help, God will be gracious and help you rebuild your shattered and broken life. He will turn it into something amazing.

In the midst of that mighty storm, things can seem pretty hopeless. The rain pelting down, the thunder shaking the foundations of all you have built and the winds ripping apart what you have spent so much time putting together. God has a marvelous plan to create something beautiful out of the broken pieces of your life. He wants only what is best for you. He, however, cannot do anything to help you until you are willing to ask Him and then let Him take over rebuilding. He is after all the Master Carpenter.

Have you ever seen a beautiful old cathedral, with its grand stained glass windows? Those windows start out as pieces of glass that had to be cut and broken into different shapes and sizes. They don't really look like much, just a bunch of pieces of glass laying around. Then the craftsmen spend much time and care to put them together just right. Of course, that's after he has cut and broken them into just the right sizes and shapes. He then carefully arranges them and solders them together and by the time he is finished, he has created a beautiful picture, that will radiate all the more, as the sun shines through it. Kind of like us, God takes our lives, ever so carefully breaks and cuts the pieces, carefully arranges them and solders them together, places them right where they need to be, to catch the light. Then as God's light, Jesus, shines in and through us we become something absolutely stunning and magnificent. Remember that, He not only created you, me and everyone, He also created the entire universe. Do you think, just maybe, He can handle putting the broken pieces of your life back together and bringing out your true beauty? He has known all along what He created you to be, even if you, yourself could not see it.

FROM DARKNESS TO LIGHT

Some days bring many unexpected things, most of us start our day with our plan for the day. We set our alarm to wake up, so that we can accomplish what we have planned. Whether it's going to work, running errands or maybe doing something special with family and/or friends. Sure, all these things are important. How about we back up for a moment, take a deep breath, and give our Father in Heaven our praise and then; here it comes, next how about we hand our day over to the One who created us and ask what He has planned for our day. What, are you crazy? I don't have time for that. I'm far too busy. I'm far too important. I have way too much I have to get done. I'm on a tight schedule. Too many people depend on me, I wouldn't want to let them down. Any of those sound familiar? Did you ever stop to consider that maybe the reason your life seems so chaotic, is because you don't put God first? Maybe the reason things seem to keep going wrong is because your plans and God's plans for you just don't match up. Would it really be so difficult to take time out, at the start of the day, to thank God for all the many blessings He has already given you? Instead, most of the time we wait till the end of the day, if at all. How about we stop first thing and thank God and give Him praise. We should be giving Him our first and our best; after all, He did give us His first and His best, His one and only Son, Jesus the Christ.

Then, instead of making it our day, our plan, our responsibility, how about we give God control over our day?

"This is the day which the Lord hath made; we will rejoice and be glad in it." *__Psalms 118:24 KJV.__* Think of how much lighter you would feel if you're not carrying the weight of the world on your shoulders. That is a burden God never intended you to bear. Jesus did, after all, say, **"Come onto me all you that labor and are heavy laden, and I shall give you rest."** *__Matthew 11:28 KJV__*, **"For my yoke is easy and my burden is light".** *__Matthew 11:30 KJV.__*

You might just be amazed at how differently things turn out. God may have some wonderful surprises waiting for you. Can you imagine how much lighter you will feel not carrying the entire weight of the world on your shoulders? After all, God never intended for you to carry such a heavy burden around with you. He is more than happy to shoulder the burden for you.

This does not mean throwing away all the responsibility and sitting down and waiting for God to personally come down from His throne in Heaven and go over the itinerary for the day with you. God has given you a wonderful guide, a comforter and counselor. The Holy Spirit is always there for you. If you are already a Christian, then the Holy Spirit is your personal guide along the journey God has mapped out for you. We just have to learn to listen and follow His directions. Too many times, we ask for direction and guidance, but we don't take the time to stop and listen to the answer. We are just too darn busy. Then we get mad at God because things always seem to go wrong. If we would just learn to listen to that 'still small voice', when the Holy Spirit is trying to tell us something and trust that God has only good things planned for us, then don't you think things would be much different.

Our part in this great adventure, is after all, to listen, be patient and to follow our guide book (the Holy Bible) and let our guide (the Holy Spirit) lead the way.

If you haven't already become a Christian and accepted the amazing free gift Jesus died to give you, well now is a great time to do so. Jesus is waiting patiently for you to come to Him. If the truth be known Jesus has been actively pursuing, you all along. He loves you dearly and wants to welcome you home and introduce you as a new creation to His Heavenly Father, God and send the Holy Spirit to guide, comfort and counsel you. He is all ready to receive you and has amazing gifts waiting for you. Gifts are by definition free. *A thing given willingly to someone without payment; a present.* **Oxford dictionaries.** Ask and you will receive the free gift of salvation. Trust and believe in Jesus, He is waiting with open arms to welcome you.

Sometimes we want to bestow something on someone, just because we love them and want them to be happy. Salvation through grace and the peace that passes our understanding are some of the gifts God has waiting for you. All you have to do is to believe in Jesus the Christ who lived, died (suffering great physical pain, emotional persecution and spiritual torment) and was then resurrected and all for you personally. If you, indeed where the only one in the entire universe that needed salvation, He would have still paid this enormous cost just for you and did. Tell God you know that you are a sinner, accept salvation through his Son Jesus (God's only begotten Son) and His suffering and sacrifice for you and allow the Holy Spirit to come and fill the vast void, the emptiness within you and comfort you and counsel you. Let God take your burdens and give you joy.

This in no way means that suddenly life is a bowl of cherries. In fact, Jesus said that, **"If you follow me the way will not be easy" and that "If the world hates you, ye know that it hated me before it hated you."** *JOHN 15:18 KJV.* The difference is that we know where we're going and how great the rewards are; we know how the story ends. All things of the world pale in comparison. When you start seeing things more thru God's eyes, you find things look a lot different. Things that once seemed huge and insurmountable, now seem much smaller.

It's like your brother comes to you, because he's cold and wants your old coat and you know that when you get home that you have other coat in the closet. Not only that, but you will be moving to a tropical island paradise and will never be cold again. You not only would want to give that coat to your brother, to keep warm for a while, you would probably want to invite him along so that he too would never

117

have to be cold again.

You are going to the greatest party ever and want to invite all your friends, family and neighbors. After all, with a great party like that the more, the merrier.

How many people trudge through their week, working long hours, maybe in a job they hate, just because they know the weekend is coming and they are going to a really cool party? If we deal with that, just for a party that only lasts a few hours, why can't we seem to endure what amounts to a short time on this planet, for an eternity of the best party ever?

When we get home to Heaven it will be better than anything you can imagine and we will have a whole eternity to enjoy it. If we could only truly grasp what awaits us and how truly short our time is here, I think we would complain less and rejoice a whole lot more. Not to mention, we would want to tell everybody so they too could come join the party. We should even be telling all of those really bad and messed up people. The ones we think, are so very much worse than us. Before you pass judgment on them, however, remember, *"For all have sinned, and come short of the glory of God". Romans3:23 KJV.* That's right, not one of us is perfect and all sin is vial to a perfect and righteous God. That is the point, after all, we all need salvation, so that we can be right with God. As much as He loves us He is perfectly holy and has no sin within Himself. As with darkness, it cannot exist where there is light. Light extinguishes the darkness. Light does not cast a shadow. If you don't believe that, light a candle or a match and then shine a flashlight directly on it. You will see the shadow of the candle or match, but the flame itself does not cast a shadow. Light does not cast a shadow. You may see a shadow from the smoke the flame makes, but not from the flame itself. Shadows are made up of darkness. Shadows are dark spots cast on a wall, ground, the floor, a place behind the object, so how could a flame create a shadow? The flame is made up of light.

God being loving and merciful does not want us to be extinguished, remember that light overtakes darkness. Where there is light, darkness cannot exist. If you go into a dark room and turn on the light switch, the room then becomes light, the darkness is gone. For this reason, God has made it possible for us to be born again, this into His wondrous light. He wants us to be creatures of light so that we can reside in heaven with Him. If we were to remain in sin, being part of the darkness, then we could not exist in God's radiant light. It is for that reason that such a great sacrifice was needed, that we can be reborn of the light and therefore exist with God, as creatures of light.

We cling so tightly to the things of this world. We seem to think that things like money, power, prestige, toys and style will make us happy. We mistakenly think these things will make us complete and give us purpose, and then we only end up feeling empty and alone. None of the things the world has to offer can ever fill that emptiness. The only thing that can make us complete is God. God has such wonderful things waiting for us. Things of this world are at best only a shadow or small glimpse of what waits for us in Heaven.

So many things in the Bible may seem to contradict themselves, from a worldly point of view. **"He that findeth his life shall lose it; and he that loseth his life for my sake shall find it".** *MATTHEW 10:39 KJV,* "**But many that are first shall be last; and the last shall be first".** *MATTHEW 19:30 KJV,* these are just a few of these. When you start building a relationship with God and really reading His Word with an open heart, He will start revealing His truth to you.

His light will overtake the darkness of this world, so that you may begin to see things as they truly are. Remember what seems big and scary in the dark, usually appears much smaller in the light. It is almost as if you had been sleepwalking through life and are finally waking up. Like you have lived your life in utter darkness and absence of warmth and have stepped out into the radiance of God's light and His loving warmth.

Sometimes when you go from utter darkness into the light, the brilliance of that light can hurt your eyes and the first thing you want to do is run back into the darkness. After all, it is the only thing you've ever known and it seems safe and comfortable. When you stand strong and decide to stay in the light, sure it may hurt for a time, but soon you will adjust and start seeing things as they truly are, not the dark shadows you have always known. Things always look different in the light. Then your perspectives on things start to change. When you look back upon that dark empty space where you once existed, it's hard to image just how blind you had been to the truth and how much you had actually been missing. You may even become angry at how much you missed in that dark place and how the darkness had you so imprisoned in fear and ignorance for so very long. Do not spend time in anger, it will only drag you back into the darkness which you have just broken free of. Instead, rejoice, thank God for the wonderful free gift He has given you and start drawing forward in the amazing light and love of God's grace.

How do we move forward? By asking God for help and guidance. Just because you are now standing in the Father's glorious light, doesn't mean that you can see everything clearly or even that you can understand what you see. Remember living for so long in darkness, you have learned only of dark things and have seen everything with a dark view. Even though you may now realize how wrong that was and how very distorted the view was, does not mean you suddenly know everything or even see everything clearly. Things will undoubtedly seem strange and foreign for some time. Find others that have gone down the same road that now lies ahead of you and start learning from them. Start making a habit of reading your Bible daily, even if it's only a line or two and ask God to help you understand what you're reading. Get in the habit of praying. What I mean by praying, is talking with God and listening for His answers. You know having a conversation and building a relationship with your Father God. You may be surprised at the ways in which God will answer you and the ways in which your life will be transformed. **"And I will walk among you, and will be your God and you shall be my people."** *LEVITICUS 26:12 KJV.* God wants to walk with you down the path He has laid out for you and talk with you and tell you how very much He loves you. God has a way of changing our hearts and our direction in ways we cannot even imagine. We only need to be willing to follow where ever He leads us, even if it sometimes seems scary. He will never lead you somewhere He cannot reach you. Stop trying to do things your way and of your own strength. God is plenty big enough to carry the load. After all, since He created the entire universe, do really think there is anything in it He cannot lift and carry? Do you really think there is any place, you can go that he cannot find and reach you?

POOR PITIFUL ME

I sit here talking with You God. You the God of the universe, trying desperately to convince You that I am not worthy of Your love. I feel much less than worthy and I am actually arguing with You, trying to convince You, what a complete screw up I am and so not worthy of Your great love and favor.

Even in doing this, I know it's the same a spitting in Your face. How completely presumptuous of me to tell You, I am not worthy of Your love and time. Standing before the burning bush, daring to argue with the GREAT I AM. The God who gave His only begotten Son that we may be redeemed. I argue and tell *You,* that surely *You* have the wrong person. Me, well, I'm just a messed up person and will surely let You down, as I let everyone around me down.

All these great gifts that You have given me, I can't even figure out how to use them properly. I seem to mess up and/or break everything I Touch. I know deeply who You are and how very much You have done for me. Even with that knowledge, there is guilt. You seem to show me such favor and awesome mercy; You speak so clearly and answer me quickly. Even if I wanted to deny Your existence I could not, because I know You and know how real You are. Yet still, I argue and barter and try to convince You that, in all Your infinite wisdom, You have somehow managed to make a huge cosmic goof, me. This is, of course, totally and utterly absurd. Still, somehow there is this feeling, at this moment in time that I will undoubtedly let You down. Of course, You know just how messed up I am. Isn't that the point? Isn't it because You knew how much I have and will continue to mess things up, that You sent Jesus to save me, to save all of us?

We certainly are not capable of saving ourselves. If we could, would that not make us more powerful than our Creator? Sitting here, knowing that this is most certainly an attack from the pit of hell itself, but somehow it still feels like it is all my fault. Yes, my fault, everything. Oh yes, everything. Everything that has ever gone wrong in the world. Everything that has ever hurt someone in any way, everything that will ever go wrong.

This is not by far, the first or only time I have felt like this. I have purposely done many things over the years to make God turn away from me. Dabbled (that may be the understatement of the millennium), in things no human ever should, pressed my luck and tested God's patience. I really do not understand at this moment as God Himself allows me to remember all the things I have done, just to spite Him. Why, He the King of Kings, the Lord of Lords, the Creator of the Universe, even bothers to waste his time on me?

Then He reminds me that nothing, that He does is ever a waste of time. He has had this all planned out since before the beginning of time. Yet, still I argue with Him and He does not strike me down. In fact, He takes the time to listen, encourage and love me. It is to me a great mystery why and in this life I may never truly understand why, but He does. He loves you just as deeply and completely. He has a great plan for you, and you don't have to make it happen, you only have to know and believe that God, the Father who loves you so very much will make it happen. They are after all, His great plans. Do we really think that we are powerful enough to change even one small part of the plan He has to save us and bring us home to be with Him?

He takes the time to listen, to converse and love me. He does and will take the time to do the same with and for you. It probably won't be the same way He talks to me. God made each of us unique and knows how best to talk to each of us individually.

Make no mistake, when I began to write this chapter I was in deep, seemingly endless despair. God allowed me to see and feel every little thing that I ever felt, I did wrong. Lately, God has been listening to me whine and complain and plead a lot. He has seen many tears streaming down my face and has comforted me and carried me through this. I truly feel that if God had not been there with me through this, that I would not be here to continue writing this book. I know that the attacks of the enemy have been great and that even with this knowledge, I feel very much unworthy.

I do not feel that I am important enough for the enemy to take notice of me, to take the time to launch such a great assault. But that my dear ones is the point, He is our Father and so loves us that in itself makes us important. Not anything we have done or could ever do will change how very much God loves all of His children, even when we don't acknowledge Him.

When you are in the midst of anguish and feel there is no hope left, no reason to go on, that is a direct attack from the pit of hell itself. If satan himself sees you as enough of a threat to launch such a great assault on you personally, that must mean you are pretty important to God and a very special part of His great plan. Take comfort in this and know how very much God your Father in Heaven loves you. He loves you enough to take the time to listen to you whine and complain, rage and cry out and yes, rejoice and sing out. He wants you to know that He always has the time to listen to all you have to say and He will never laugh at you, but He loves to laugh with you and loves to make you laugh. Remember He love to give us, Joy.

EMPTY HANDS

God has so much in store for us and He has many wonderful gifts, but first we need to be willing and ready to accept them. We have to be willing to have empty hands and open arms, otherwise, how can we possibly receive what He is so freely giving us.

Remember the story in The Bible about the rich man who asked Jesus what he needed to do to follow Him. I'm not including that scripture because of its length, however, very much encourage you to look it up, ***Matthew 19:16-22.*** Jesus told the man to go and sell everything he owned and give the money to the poor and "then come follow Me". Do you really think that Jesus was being mean and spiteful? Do you think that Jesus just simply wanted the man to be poor and that we all must be poor to follow Him and be closer to God? Jesus knew this man had a heart problem, not a money problem. He knew this man loved his money and possessions more than God. Well, when we go to God with our hands full and so much clutter around us that we can't even see where we're going, let alone our Father standing right in front of us. He only wants us to get the junk out of the way so He can reach us. I know a number of good Christians who are rich and who are poor and everywhere in between. God only wants what is best for us. To some, money can be a great gift and they use it wisely, for some, it may be a major stumbling block. Likewise, for some being poor is a great gift and they use this wisely, while for others being poor may do more harm than good. One example that strikes me, was "Mother Theresa". Being poor only seemed to strengthen her. If she had in fact been wealthy she may still have been a good person, but she may not have been able to help so very many. Maybe she would have been self-center and cruel. Only Gods in His infinite wisdom truly knows. She saw things in a different light because of her position in life, in ways that many of us may never understand. I see things the way I do because of all my life experiences, thank God for that.

There is a local man who owns a well-respected company and probably has more money than most realize. This man is very humble and helps many people on a regular basis. He gives his time, his talent and his money. I have never personally heard him boast or put anyone down. God continues to bless him and he continues to bless all those around him.

God, Himself, will help us clean up all the clutter, but we have to take the first step and ask Him. In the story of, "The rich Young Ruler", **And a certain ruler asked Him, saying Good Master, what must I do to inherit eternal life? <u>Luke 18:18 KJV.</u>**   He seemed like he wanted to follow God, but as soon as he was asked to get rid of that which was cluttering his life, we quickly see what was most important to him, his money and his possessions, his tune quickly changed. This man, if you remember, was also very boastful. He when questioned quickly made a point of saying in front of everyone there, that he was a good and righteous man and had kept **all** of Gods commandments **all** of his life. I would be hard pressed to believe that was actually the case. That would mean he was righteous. The Bible tells us that, **"As it is written, there is none that is righteous, no, not one".** *ROMANS 3:10 KJV.*

If you don't know the Ten Commandments, then now would be a great time to look them up there near the front of the Bible in *Exodus 20:3-17 KJV.* The Ten Commandments seem to be a pretty strict set of laws and for any of us to keep all of them, all of our lives are pretty much impossible. Especially when you truly understand all of the commandments. Like, **"Thou shall not kill"**, *EXODUS 20:13 KJV.* Which, if you understand the extent of what this commandment says, if you have ever hated someone, then you have already committed murder in your heart. Ouch, so have you ever hated anyone, then by God's law you are a murderer. **"Thou shall not commit adultery"**, *EXODUS 20:14 KJV.* If you have ever lusted after someone you are not married to, then you have already committed adultery in your heart. How about, **"Thou shall not steal"**, *EXODUS 20:15 KJV.* It doesn't have to be anything big. Maybe you took a pen from work or swiped a cookie without asking. That would be stealing. That is just three of the ten commandments. Do you really think that you or anyone could keep all of God's perfect laws, all the time, for your entire life? Not the rich man that went to Jesus claiming to have kept them, nor the guy sitting on 'death row', nor you or I. We are all dirty, sinned covered people, that is why Jesus came to pay the price, for all the things we have

129

done and ever will do. That is why we need to let go of things and let God clear out all the clutter, so that we can receive what He has for us.

MIRACLES

Many times we ask, "Does God still perform miracles today?" Well, the answer is a resounding, YES! So much of the time we just don't recognize them when we see them. With so many miracles packed into the Bible, we think that the miracles surely must be all used up. I am here to tell you that God absolutely still loves His children (us) and still reigns down miracles on us. Too often we brush these awesome miracles aside as coincidences. We think that we don't deserve them. Surely, God won't bless such a rebellious lot, such as ours. If God only blessed the ones who deserved blessing, then do you really think anyone (even the great men and women of the Bible) would get blessed and receive miracles. Miracles are not something that we can earn. They come out of God's endless love for us. They are one of the many ways He shows us just how very much He loves us. They are a way for God to reveal part of His nature to us. There are many different kinds of miracles. Like the parting of the 'red sea', that was pretty big. If you were standing there by a great body of water, with Pharaoh charging forward, ready to wipe you out of existence and all of a sudden the waters parted right in front of your eyes, that would be pretty hard to deny. *EXODUS 14:16*.

God is the same yesterday, today, tomorrow and forever. He never changes, even when we do. He wants to bring us back to Him and build a relationship with us. Since God never changes, then it is reasonable to stay that He still does miracles.

In my church, we have been studying Exodus. Through this teaching, I have come to see God's love for His rebellious children in a whole new light, the blinding light, the light of God's eternal love for us, His beloved children. God goes to great extremes to save us and bring us back to Him. Time after time, while learning more about God's true nature, I think how blessed are we that someone like me or you, is not in charge. Personally, I would have thrown in the towel a long time ago.

The children of Israel cry out to God to save them and free them from their bondage. When God sends them a deliverer, Moses, what do they do at the first sign of trouble? They turn on Moses and tell him to leave them alone, they tell God's messenger they were better off before he came and told those who enslaved them that they have nothing to do with this man. What is God's response? Does He turn away and say fine get yourselves out of this mess? Does He get mad and punish them or simply destroy them and start over? No, He is a loving and patient Father. God Continues to perform more and more greater miracles. He totally debunks all of the Egyptian Gods. Repeatedly He shows His grace and mercy to His children, whom He dearly loves. Time after time and plague after plague both the Egyptians and the Israelites ignore what God is doing. Even after all of the wonders God did in the desert, still His children spoke against Him.

Yes, children are a wonderful blessing, but do think that just maybe God had a second purpose. Maybe God is also showing us through them, a glimpse of what He deals with. How we, many times, like our own children we have temper tantrums and just have to have our own way.

Any who, if we simply open our eyes and take a good look at things, then we would see that our world is full of God's great miracles, large and small. By our standards anyway. There really are no small miracles. A miracle by definition is *"an unusual or wonderful event that is believed to be caused by the power of God."* **_Merriam-Webster's dictionary._** God always gives us his very best. He does nothing halfway. It's not in His nature to do less than His best.

I have personally seen so very many awesome things happen that there is absolutely no doubt in my mind, that God still pours out on us a cup overflowing with miracles and the cups never empties or runs dry.

The most recent of these happened just today. We have spent the last few months trying to sell my mother in laws house, so that we could move her much closer to us. She presently lives approximately an hour and a half way and her health is getting progressively worse (she has Parkinson's disease) and we live in Northern Michigan. Winter can make that drive much longer and far more treacherous. We have also spent these last months trying to find a house for her to live in that is close. We had a couple of people look at her house, but that was all it amounted to and every time we would find something closer, someone else would buy it before we had a chance to make an offer.

Through this process, we would pray and say "God, we know you have a house for her, please lead us to it". We were close to taking her house back off the market, when finally, an offer was made. The people didn't even come to look at it, they lived in another state. So finally, a light at the end of the tunnel. Still, there were obstacles to overcome before the offer could go through. In the mean time, we ramp up the search for a house for her to move to. We find a house that seems perfect and only about 2 miles away from us. Before we can make the offer the bank accepts another offer on that house. We call our Realtor (who by the way is nothing short of awesome) and she again goes to work searching for the right house, in the right location. We narrow the search to just the town we live in and Linda (our awesome Realtor) finds a house that is not only closer by a half mile, but is also newer. Once again before we can make an offer, not one but two offers are made on that house. This time I just really felt that God had something better for her, but getting a bit nervous. We were within less than two weeks of closing on the sale of her house and we still had not found anything for her to move into. My husband and I talked and agreed that we would move her in with us and what things we would need to do to make that happen. Then we told our 16-year-old about Granny moving in and the changes that we would have to make. Though our son, no doubt, loves his

Granny, he was not at all happy about her living with us. Right after that discussion (the next day or two, I believe) Linda calls us with another house, which she thinks would be perfect. We talk and decide to go ahead and look at the house with the two offers on it, just in case and the house Linda told us about. We go after church meet Linda at the house with the two offers. It was not a bad house, but none of us (my husband, myself or Linda) were very excited about. Both Linda and I are however very excited about looking at the other house. The night before I showed my father in law pictures of both the houses online and he said "I really think that's the one", about the other house.

Off we go, excited, yet kind of afraid to 'get our hopes up'. We all get there and nothing had been plowed or shoveled and we had just had a fair amount of snow. Thankfully, we had not tried to bring my in-laws with, there is no way my mother-in-law could have gotten through all that snow. We all waded through the snow and when we got inside, all were amazed. This place had everything we wanted and more. There were some minor things that would need fixing, but this house would be perfect. This house is even bigger than what she is presently living in and she really did not wish to part with any of her things. Now the next step. Getting the offer in before someone else does. There was a hold up with the bank, we were going into the weekend and the closing on her house, the house she presently lived in, was the following Tuesday. Tuesday morning my husband goes to his mother's for the closing, ends up having to wait till after the bank is closed to get the check, so it cannot be deposited till the next day. Our Realtor submits our offer on the house. My awesome husband, stays overnight at his mother's (to save a couple more hour and half drives), so he can deposit the check and go and talk to Linda. The next morning after he leaves the office and within less than ten minutes, Linda our awesome Realtor, calls my husband to tell him she just heard back from the bank on the house and the offer had been accepted. My husband and I went to meet with Linda our realtor and he signed the paperwork, which was set up to have the closing 28 days from the date the offer was made. Well, when the paperwork came back, HUD changed it to 45 days. My mother-in-law was already paying rent on the house she had lived in for over 30 years, since the deal had already closed. We were needless to say getting a bit edgy, needing to get her moved. A couple days later our realtor again called us, this time, to tell us that according to the paperwork from the title company we may be able to close the deal on the house much sooner, within a couple of weeks. We had gotten our miracle. We get yet another call from our realtor letting us know she checked with the title company and we could close on the new house as soon as we wished. Within about two weeks we closed on the house and had my mother in law moved into the new house. There is actually much more to this story, but that would take up many more pages.

We have been praising God for this amazing gift, this awesome miracle. God, once again has shown us His great love. This miracle has touched many lives already. Those already mentioned and those who have personally heard me tell the story of this amazing event. God is smiling down saying "I had it all under control, right from the beginning. You just need to learn to trust Me a little more". God, I am trying and little by little learning. Thank You Father, for understanding and being so very patient with me.

By the way, Linda, our awesome Realtor, is a believer. I truly believe that having a good Christian working with us to find a house and push this deal through makes all the difference in the world. God uses people around us. Thank you God, for putting this wonderful woman there to help us through this time.

I still get a bit nervous about things, sometimes, as you may have gathered from what I have told you. The difference is not losing any sleep and seeing things in a totally different light now. Knowing that things are in Gods, very capable hands and that it will all work out according to His plan, helps me to rest much easier. I don't have to know everything. Just knowing and trusting in the One who has the plan, makes all the difference. It doesn't matter how big or how small things are, God has our best interest at heart.

Since He is the One who created this great universe, don't you think He is capable of making sure things go the way He planned? Our plans may not always work out the way we want them to, especially when we refuse to listen to God. You know when we throw caution to the wind; refuse to hear that 'still small voice', inside us telling to follow the plan laid out before us. Sometimes, as the Bible tells us, we just need to, *"Be still, and know that I am God"*. **_PSALMS 46:10._** *He* is there all the time watching over us and His love for us is immeasurable.

Still human being and tending to doubt and sometimes still trying to follow my own plans, as many of us do, there are those times I fall flat on my face. He knows this about us; He does not expect us to be perfect. He does, however, expect us to try to do our best. To try to listen and follow His instructions to the best of our abilities and to trust our Creator. How do we do that? We read the instruction manual (the Bible), we pray (talk to God) and earnestly seek and praise Him.

I have told you about one of the "big" miracles in my life, now let me tell you about one of the seemingly small miracles. When we were getting ready to move back to Michigan, my husband was already in Michigan, helping with his mother and trying to find us a house to buy. Well, there was this list of things I wanted in order to move back to Michigan, from Oregon. It wasn't a very long list, but I was pretty set on certain things. One of them was needing a good church close to where we would be living. I had been praying about that a lot. My husband knew nothing about my list. While we were talking on the phone one night, without me saying anything, my husband started telling me about this church he had been told about, I couldn't believe it. Could this be an answer to yet another prayer, one that I had just started asking God about the night before? It seemed too good to be true. My husband gave me their website and I went online and checked it out. This had to be the church I was asking for. It was exactly what we needed, right location, only a couple of miles from the house we would be living in; a good, Bible believing church and so much more. Looking back on it now, this was absolutely the answer to that prayer. One more amazing miracle from God, yet another answer to prayer.

Truly God does miracles all the time. They are just part of who He is. We serve an incredibly amazing and loving God. When did we stop recognizing and appreciating all the amazing things He does for us? Too many times, we pray about something and then brush the answers off as, just another coincidence, instead of thanking Him for the wonderful things He does. Thank you God for everything.

A RELATIONSHIP WITH GOD

I have said and very much believe God wants us to involve Him in every aspect of our lives and turn to Him with all of our troubles and yes our accomplishments, big and small. That doesn't mean whine and complain constantly. That means to earnestly turn to God. That may even mean crying out and asking God to show us the why, and being ready to trust Him when He doesn't immediately give us an answer. We can always go back to the throne and ask again later. Sometimes, however, as the song says, sometimes we need to, "thank God for unanswered prayers". Only too often He doesn't give us what we ask for because He knows it will hurt us or because He has something much better for us or maybe the timing just isn't right.

Our Pastor, this past Sunday was giving a very heartfelt sermon. After last Friday's shooting of 20 innocent elementary school children, hearing my pastor say "I don't want prayer back in schools", really got me. I had to sit back shut up and listen. I knew he certainly must have a point to this statement. After a short pause, he continued. He said that, first of all if we were to put prayer back in schools in this day and age that we would have to include other religions.

Secondly, and I feel more importantly that as Christians we are to pray all the time, everywhere we are and go. In our schools, at work, in the park, at the grocery store, while we're driving. We can pray silently, everywhere we are. The government cannot regulate or stop us from praying silently. The fact is that God wants us to pray. Prayer is talking to Him. We try to make it about ceremony and ritual, but really prayer is about building a relationship with our Father God. It's about talking to Him, asking Him questions and listening for the answers. In short getting to know Him.

If you are trying to build a relationship with someone, what is the first thing you do? That's right you start talking and asking questions, so you can learn more about them and they, in turn, can learn about you. The more you talk with them, the more intimate the relationship becomes, the deeper and stronger the bond becomes.

Sometimes praying can simply mean being in the presence of God, quietly listening and enjoying being close to Him. Words are not always necessary.

Have you ever fallen in love, do you remember how that can feel? Sometimes you just simply want to be close to the one you love, not say a word. Besides God knows your heart, He knows your needs, He knows you better than you know yourself. Yes, pour out your heart to God, plead and intercede for others, yell, unload and for heaven's sake worship Him. Once in a while though, just let Him know how very much you love Him, just be in His presence and feel His immense love. Sometimes you cannot put into words the things you want and need to say. I, at times like that, try to, **"be still and** know that I Am God". *__Psalm 46:10 KJV__* and Listen for that, "**still small voice**". *__1 Kings 19:12__*. When you become still and quiet and just listen, when you let all of life's noise fade away, that is when it becomes easier to hear that "still small voice".

God has a wonderful sense of humor. Like when I was going through some exceptionally difficult times, awhile back and God was giving me signs to help me through it. He gave me a sign one day and it wasn't until the next day on the way to church that I realized what had happened and that it was, in fact, a sign from God. I then heard an almost audible voice say, "here's your sign", and began to laugh. Figure everything good comes from God, therefore, doesn't it make sense that God would have a sense of humor. Things that are truly good come from God. He invented laughter and enjoys making us laugh, laughter is truly a gift.

One night while helping with youth group, just sitting watching these wonderful teens talking and laughing, it hit me. As wonderful as that was, how much better it will be in Heaven. Think about it, being able to laugh, truly laugh as long as you like and never getting tired or ending up with sore stomach muscles from laughing so long and hard.

Back to relationship. Don't get me wrong, I am in no way claiming to be a relationship expert. You don't have to be an expert to figure out a few of the basics. Overall God makes it pretty simple to understand what kind of relationship He wants with you. He, like any good parent, wants to be involved in your life. He wants to know about the big things and the small things, what makes you happy and what upsets you. He also wants this relationship to be a two-way street. He wants you to listen when He speaks to you and acknowledge that He is God and worthy of all praise. He, however, will never force you to do anything you don't want to do. That would just destroy any relationship that existed. You cannot force someone to love you. It just doesn't work that way. At that point, it isn't love, it's fear and you have become a slave. God does not want, nor does He need slaves.

In any good relationship, there is give and take. When we love someone, we want to do things that make the other person happy. This does not mean, however that we ignore things done wrong. When someone makes a mistake and we truly care about them, we want to help them correct that mistake so it doesn't mess other things up. If a mistake is not corrected it can change everything that happens after it. Especially if we don't even realize that we have made that mistake. When you love and care about someone you want to help them realize and correct the mistake. Not to wave it in their face and say, "Ha, ha you got that wrong", but because you care and want them to be happy, you want them to know the difference between what is right and what is wrong. Knowing that could be the difference in how they later make decisions. When things are done wrong, those decisions could potentially hurt them and those around them. When you love and care about someone, you want only what

143

is best for them.

There was a time many years ago that my boyfriend, at the time and I were driving around. He was driving much too fast. I made a comment about his speed and he started to insist that he was doing the speed limit, which was 25mph. In fact, he was going closer to 50mph. I looked over at the gauges and realized that he was looking at the wrong gauge. He wasn't purposely speeding. I pointed out what the problem was, he looked and realized that in fact he was going by the wrong gauge and corrected his speed. If nothing had been said, for fear of hurting his feelings or offending him, he may have ended up getting a speeding ticket and worse yet causing an accident. I said something because I cared, the problem was corrected and no trouble came from it. He may have been slightly embraced for a moment, but no one got hurt. A little embarrassment was far outweighed by what could have potentially been a life changing accident. Do you think that would have made anyone very happy? Of course not.

You see when God corrects us, even if we don't like it at the time, it is not out of any kind of malice. He does not want to see us fail. He really does want us to be happy, sometimes that may mean making us uncomfortable for a while. He even puts up with the temper tantrums we throw. He corrects us, because He loves us enough to want what's best for us. Once again, thank You for putting up with all my self-centered temper tantrums God, and I have had many. Thank You for being so very patient with me.

We don't always see the troubles that lie right in front of us, but Father God does. He, goes over and above to correct us in a very loving way. Sometimes He just steps back and lets us make a few mistakes, because it is the only way we can learn. We end up with some cuts and scrapes out of the deal, but the consequences could be far worse if we are left completely to our own devices. God is never more than a prayer away. He always listens and always answers, we don't always hear or pay much attention to those answers. How many times in a relationship does the other person try to tell you something to help you and instead you just get mad or ignore them all together? Have you ever tried to help someone by pointing out a mistake, only to have them get mad at you or blame you for their mistake? It is very hurtful, especially if you were truly just trying to help. How do you think our Father God feels, when we do the same to Him? When we blame Him for all that is wrong in our lives and all that is wrong with the world. That is very hurtful. He is very loving and very patient. Apologizing when we realize what we've done is at very least just the right thing to do and shows God that we love Him and are remorseful for our mistakes.

Relationships are seldom easy, but good ones are so very worthwhile. God feels that we are very much worth it. When you care deeply, you are willing to risk much for the sake of the other, just because you love them and want what's best for them. God feels that the relationship with you is that important. He risked everything for you. He sent His only, beloved Son to die for you. Yes, you are that important to Him, that He gave everything to save you, knowing that you may still reject Him. You know what, He loves fiercely, He loves deeply and He loves completely. That is a kind of love that we are not even capable of.

A GRAND NEW ADVENTURE

Talk is cheap, but action is priceless. My husband and I finally decided in stop making excuses and trust God. We felt that we were being lead to head south. Didn't really know why or exactly where. We bought a motor home and head out on the road, putting our trust in God's plan.

Of course, there was a little more than that to it. It started many years ago, my husband and I started talking how we both strongly felt that God had much more in store for us. Off and on we would talk on the subject. Life always seemed to find things to distract us. The kids, school, our jobs, friends and even obligations at church. You name it there was always something. There we go again, caught up in life and forgetting what we felt so strongly was God's will in our life.

Finally, all these years later, I started thinking, it was time to let go and let God have control. It was time to just go. I didn't know where or how and I certainly didn't think my husband would go for jumping off a cliff like this. Trying to brush it aside and not to think about, did not work. Just staying on the same old path wasn't going to work.

I had a job that I could not leave. We needed the insurance because my husband had bladder cancer and then was diagnosed with diabetes, as well. There was no way to leave my job. I was obligated to my clients, who I loved dearly. Everyone including friends, family, and even some of my clients were saying "You need to leave your job". That it was literally killing me. The stress was definitely taking its toll. More often than not, I would be it tears on my way to my clients and I was turning into a real ogre at home. We needed the insurance. There was no way to leave this job.

During this same time frame, all within a few months, my mother in law was dying. I was dealing doctors and nurses, and broaching the subject of putting her on Hospice, to my husband. Everything appeared to be coming apart at the seams. My mother in law, whom I loved dearly passed, June 2, 2014. We flew our daughter out from Oregon and our 2 sons from Utah to see their granny for the last time, before she died. Our daughter had to go home after about a week, so when her Granny died we flew her back again, this time with her boyfriend. We had not physically met him yet, though I had many wonderful conversations with him on the phone. This was a blessing straight from God. What an incredible young man he is.

The boys made it here just before my mother in law passed. By that time, she was less than coherent. It was hardest on our oldest son. He had not been able to see her for a few years, he felt a lot of guilt. I am pretty sure it was for his sake that she held on as long as she did. It was right after the boys came to see her that she passed peacefully in her sleep. My eldest son, told me that while he was sitting out in the garage after she passed, that he saw a butterfly, fly from the house over towards him and then off over the trees. He told me it was like she was saying good bye and that he had even planned on getting a tattoo of a butterfly with her name as the body. What a beautiful way for God to show His love for our son. This also deeply touched my heart.

We got through all the turmoil and managed to have some wonderful family time with the kids. It was kind of like having a family reunion.

Soon after the kids went back home, my husband had the last of a series of cancer surgeries. It was after that surgery that I found out the company I worked for had removed my husband from my insurance. It was then that I was finally able to make the decision. It was time to leave my job.

Everything was falling into place. The things I had been holding on to for so long, my manna was getting pretty stinky. The house and land that I so loved, were now beginning to feel more like a chain around my neck, weighing me down. The job which had provided for us financially was making me tired and literally sick. Truth be known, it was probably heading me toward divorce, because I was becoming such an ogre. These things that at one time had been such an incredible blessing, were now turning into major burdens. Once again, like God's children wondering in the desert, I was clinging to things. It was time to let go. God gave His children manna to feed them, telling them not to save it. For that day, it would feed and bless them. When they didn't heed God's word and held on to it till morning, it rotted and became stinky. It was the same with the blessings in my life, that I was clinging to. God wants us to trust Him for all the things in life that we need, He will provide for us, if we let him.

Now was the time to let go and let God. Trust in Him and know that He loves us and will provide all that we need. He had me in a place where, trusting Him was pretty much the only option. In fact, God had put a burning desire in me to Strike out on his path, to let it all go and see what great adventure He had in store for us.

This had been a time of absolute chaos in my life. My husband's health issues, quitting my job, trying to clean out my mother in laws house and figure out where to store everything. Plus, thinning things out at our house, especially food. We had three freezers, store bought food and a ton of home canned stuff. We couldn't just leave it all there. Surely the can goods would freeze and explode and I didn't want three freezers running while we were gone for the winter. Having left my job, provided the time I needed to do the things I needed to do. God was doing great things in our lives during this chaotic time. He was opening doors and preparing us for a grand new adventure. After talking to my husband about what I felt God wanted us to do and him agreeing, we started searching for a motor home. Figuring we would never be able to afford one. If this truly was God's will, He would have to make it happen. Sure enough, before long we found an older motor home. It was thirty-four feet long and in great shape. The best part of all, we only paid $1500.00 for it.

It was during this time that God sent a wonderful young woman across our path. She was working trying to better herself and had just rented a place, but had nothing. No food, no furniture, she needed almost everything. We had a lots of things that I just wanted to go to good use. My husband and I were able to give her everything from food to furniture. Including a freezer half full a food, a bed and bedding, dishes, Christmas decorations and even a car. This amazing young woman was so gracious in accepting our help, what a blessing. Giving is one thing, but I know from personal experience that excepting help can be very hard. It was such a joy and blessing getting to help this young woman. It also allowed us to finish cleaning out my mother in laws house and thin things out at our own house before going on the road. We also were able to donate multiple loads of furniture, clothes, nick knacks and a lot of other stuff to places like the food pantry thru our church, Women's Resource Center and Goodwill. I never imagined we would be able to help so many. To me, it's kind of like getting to play Santa and of course, it is what the Bible says we are to do. **"For the poor shall never cease out of the land: therefore, I command thee, saying, Thou shalt open thine hand wide unto thy brother, to thy poor, and to thy needy, in thy land."** *__Deuteronomy 15:11 KJV__*

Now one thing I need to make clear at least it is the way things seem to go for us, is when you're doing God's will expect things to go

151

haywire. Everything was falling into place, we were getting close to the time to leave and sure enough, things started to go wrong. We needed to get the brakes fixed on the motor home and get new tires, before we started loading the things we needed to take with. It was now the end of October and we needed to get on the road before the snow flew. Motor homes and snow are not a good combination. We brought the motor home into the local garage and they were supposed to have it ready in about a week. That was cutting close but still acceptable. It took longer than expected for them to start work on it. Then, they found another problem and they were having troubles locating a part that was needed. We still had to get new tires for the motor home and were having trouble finding a place that would do tires for our 34-foot motor home. During this time, we had a pretty good snow storm come thru and we're in Northern Michigan, a little town called Buckley. My husband was ready to give up and just stay thru the winter. OK God, if you want us to go, it's up to you. Well long story short, the motor home got fixed (costing less than expected, we were on a limited budget), we found a place to put new tires on the motor home, and again they were cheaper than expected, the snow melted and we were able to leave by, about late November, shortly before Thanksgiving. We headed south. When you're doing God's will, you're making the enemy mad, so, of course, things are going to go haywire. I actually expect things to go wrong, that's how I know we're on the right track to doing God's will.

We finally headed out and everything seemed like it was finally on track, as we got further south, heading out of Michigan, the weather started going downhill. Now at least we were on the road heading in the right direction, trying to follow God's plan. As we got into Indiana the winds were picking up and the roads are getting pretty rough. At one point we heard something and I could see something flapping on my side of the motor home. My husband pulled off the freeway to check and see what had happened. When he got back in, he told me that not only had we lost the awning off the motor home, his brand new fat tire bike was gone. That's right, between the winds and the tough roads it was probably laying on the side of the freeway a few miles back. God, please at least don't let it be to beat up and let someone who can use it find it, we're not going back.

We ended up pulling off, a day or so after the awning and bike incident, to get a bite to eat and gas up. Low and behold more challenges. We had no blinkers. A 34-foot motor home, towing a 16-foot car hauler with a jeep on it, we needed to be able to signal to make lane changes. I called around to find a garage that could do the work on the motor home and had the time. Finally, a number of phone calls later, I located one a couple miles up the road. Next problem, it's late afternoon and everyone is closing early because the next day is, Thanksgiving. Guess what, they can't start to work on it til Friday the day after Thanksgiving. The guy at the garage is nice enough to let us park next to the garage on the street and plug the motor home into their power supply. So, we have lights and that's about it. The furnace isn't working and it going to be a cold night. The fridge was braced up with a bar, because of the beating the motor home took on the road. At least it works, though we have nothing to speak of for food. Body heat and lots of blankets got us through that cold night and into Thanksgiving morning. Cold, hungry and stranded, we had noticed a sign for a community meal up the road. We thought of going to check it out, but it didn't appear that anything was going on there, no sign of anyone there. While walking back, a car pulled over, it just so happened that it was the people putting on the dinner and they directed us to where it was. They were bringing yet another load of food down so they had no room in the car. One of them did, however, come back to walk us down. We were still having trouble finding the right place. We got there just before they were ready to shut down. We were however welcomed in, they got us both plates of food and had us sit and eat with them. We had hot food, good company and great conversation. Then to top it off, they packed up the rest of the food (there was still a lot) and drove us and all that food back to where the motor home was parked. What an amazing way to spend the Holiday. Not something I would have chosen, but I wouldn't change it for the world. I was so happy and very thankful. We had enough food to last for a while and memories to last a lifetime. Warrior, Alabama and the wonderful people there, will always have a place in my heart.

I did say this was going to be a great adventure and we were just getting started. As our trip progressed I took more and more pictures to post on Facebook so friends and family could see where we were and what was going on. There were pictures of birds, trees, malls and scenery. Most of the pictures were wonderful.

Then the next trial came our way. We were staying at an RV park near Robertsdale, Alabama and once again it got cold. This time, however, it got down to about 10 degrees. When we woke up, it was 39 degrees inside the motor home, remember the furnace did not work. We had bought a couple of space heaters, while in Warrior, but they just couldn't keep up with the cold. I went outside as I had been doing to spray my hair and brush it out and well, my hair froze. I had to go inside to let my hair thaw so I could get the brush thru it.

My husband graciously decided that it was time to check out Mississippi. Off we went to spend a couple nights in a nice warm hotel in Mississippi. It was wonderful. The scenery was beautiful and the people were kind and laid back. We were enjoying the adventure.

Well, the second night we were there, my husband woke me up at 3am, I could hear a loud sound, but I was not awake enough to make sense of it. Then my husband told me to call 911, the jeep was on fire. That woke me up the rest of the way. Sure enough 3 o'clock in the morning, I look out the hotel window and see the jeep burning. Time to call 911 and shut myself in the bathroom so the dispatcher could hear me. The horn on the jeep was going off continuously, and it was really loud. Finally, able to get across to her what the situation was, she said, "mame, I'm sending the fire department out. They'll be there shortly." As we were waiting and watching, our only transportation burn up, my husband went outside to wait for the fire department to arrive, it seemed to be taking an awfully long time. He saw flashing lights around the corner and when he went to see what was going on, found out they had gone to a different fire. They didn't have any way to know that there was another vehicle burning in the same hotel parking lot and they went to it. My husband flagged them down, by that time the fire was pretty much out. Yes, this actually happened. You just can't make this stuff up. They said they suspected foul play. Two vehicle fires in the same parking lot at the same time, at 3 o'clock in the morning, rather suspicious. So there we were, a couple hour drive from the motor home and a long way from home.

The jeep so we thought, was toast. As the morning progressed and we had time to calm down, my amazing husband decides, what the heck, and tries to start the jeep. By nothing short of a miracle it started. Thank you Jesus. It started, we were not going to have to replace the Jeep. We did, however, have to replace the windshield, on Saturday. Yeah, every place I called told me, they couldn't get to it any earlier than Tuesday or Wednesday. Finally, after calling countless places and leaving messages with a couple of them, one calls me back and says they can come out that day, but will have to charge extra. We had them come. The extra fee was cheaper than spending a few more nights in a hotel. Thank you Jesus. Well not only did they come out and do a splendid job but they were wonderful Christian men. We had a great conversation about God and the Bible, then before leaving they prayed for us. Once again things ended with me feeling good about things and that we were exactly where we were supposed to be. God does work in some of the most interesting ways, when we just let Him. My husband did have to do some rewiring and there was now a lot more air flow on my side of the Jeep, especially for as cold as it was, but it still ran pretty darn good.

If we start looking at things through different eyes, start seeing things more from Gods perspective, then the dark times seem a whole lot brighter. We could have been and probably should have been stranded. The Jeep was on fire for quite a while. By the grace of God alone, not only did we make it back to the motor home, but we are still driving it. It's been over a year since the fire.

Don't get me wrong, when our jeep caught fire and was burning, I freaked out. After all, I am human. The trick isn't to never react; the trick is not to let your emotions control you. Take a breath and remember, God, our loving Father is at that moment and always, in control. He knows who you are (by name), He knows where you are and He knows what you need. You just have to remember to trust Him. He will never leave, nor forsake you. He has only good things for you. It is the enemy that wants you to believe otherwise. When

157

we "Let go and let God", nothing is impossible. Our jeep burned right before our very eyes and once I got passed the, "It's the end of world as I know it", reaction and remembered that God had very thing under control, things didn't seem so terrible and actually became a blessing.

While we were living in our motor home in Alabama, money was starting to become a bit scarce. We only had a limited amount of funds when we left Michigan. We really couldn't afford to go do much. We started spending a lot of time at the 'club house', at the RV park. I am so thankful for that. We started to get to know the couple who helped the park owner. We ended up becoming great friends with Shirley and Jerry. They are probably some of the best friends I have ever had. We were able to be there for them when they went through difficult times and we even got to know some of their family. She and I still keep in touch by phone and on Facebook. I wouldn't trade their friendship for anything. Thank you God for bringing them into our lives. We were also blessed with getting to know the park owner, another wonderful man of God. We started going to the weekly potlucks and met many of the other people staying there. If money had not been running so low, restricting our ability to go do things, we may never have gotten to meet so many wonderful new people. What seemed at the time to be such a restriction, turned out to be another amazing blessing? God can use even what appears to be the worst of circumstances, to do wonderful things in our lives.

God knows our flaws, he knows our miss giving's and weaknesses and He already has a plan in place to have things work out for the best, even if we don't know what that plan is. We don't have to know everything, we don't have to control everything, we just have to understand that we know the One who does.

By the way, this is coming straight from a good old fashioned, 'control freak'. I really don't like feeling like things are out of my control. It makes me very uncomfortable. I just don't like it. This has and continues to be a "thorn in my flesh", that was very hard for me to admit at first and I may always battle with it. As with all things, God knows this about me and you know what, He loves anyway. In the midst of these situations, I remind myself that He, the God of the universe is in control, so I don't have to be. It lifts a huge burden off my shoulders when I hand things over and let God take the reins of this wagon train. Let Him guide me through this vast desert we call life. Sometimes the best way to take control, is just to hand it over to God. He's not going to leave you stranded, alone and hungry. He's got your back.

Do I know where this road will take me. Of course not, we never really do. If we had known about the challenges we would face on this journey, we may have changed our plans. You know what, we would have missed out a so many wonderful things. Letting go of all the things God had already given me was infinitely more difficult than I could have imagined. Looking back now I AM SO VERY GLAD that we decided to listen to what God was telling us and go.

Not everyone will set out on this kind of a journey. This was something God set in the hearts of myself and my husband. For a long time, we had both felt that God had much more is store for us. Now we are just starting to discover a small part of that plan. Though in some ways petrified, I am at the same time excited to see where God is taking us. No matter where we end up, just so long as we're doing our best to follow his will and allow our hands to be empty that we may receive what He has for us, things will turn out for the best. Trust Father God, He after all knows exactly what he is doing.

As you may have gathered from reading this book, I am not the most eloquent writer in the world. I am definitely not a Bible scholar, stopping often to look up Bible verses. None of us are perfect by any measure. That is however the point, God does not expect us to be perfect. He knows that on our own, we have a great capacity to flat out mess things up, in His loving kindness He sent Jesus to set things right. He sent Jesus to be born, walk among us, teach us and pay the enormous price for all of our sins.

What would you do to save someone you truly love? Would you suffer and die? Would you allow yourself to be beaten, tortured, wrongly accused and be put to a horrible death just to save them? **"Greater love hath no man than this, that he would lay down his life for his friends".** ***JOHN 15:13 KJV.*** Knowing full well that they would not appreciate what you've done. In fact, that they would probably turn on you and deny you even exist. I don't know anyone that could honestly say that they would be willing to make that kind of sacrifice, even for their closest friends or family members. It's just not in our nature. Sure, we are willing to sacrifice if the cost isn't too high, if we don't have to be too uncomfortable or give up too much. That kind of a sacrifice for a wicked, spiteful, self-involved person, who won't even acknowledge your existence, now that's another story. That is exactly what Jesus did for us. He didn't wait for us to get everything right, He gave up His life while we still hated Him.

I am just one of many who fall into this category, willing to give up just so much. At the end of the day, I have a warm bed to go home to, food in the fridge and have people who are there for me. I'm really not giving up that much. I am pretty wimpy when it comes to dealing with being truly uncomfortable or sacrificing a whole lot. Even this book took far longer than it should have, because I didn't want to sacrifice too much time and give up too much to finish it. Sometimes it's really hard to get over ourselves.

My prayer for you in reading this book, is that it will help you see things in a new light. May you look at the world and your life through new eyes and see the many blessing that God has given you. Maybe you will be able to let go of the things holding you down, so that you can experience the wonderful adventure and great blessings God has in store for you. AMEN.

THINK ABOUT ME

Think about me when you hug your children
When they fall and you feel their pain
Think of me when your baby cries
And your comforting seems in vain
Think about me, when your baby takes his very first step
And when she speaks her very first word
When they curse at you and mock you
Or when they learn a brand new game
Think of how you wish to protect them
From every hurt and every pain
Think of how you must allow them
To make their own mistakes
Face their own shame
Think of all the lessons
That they would never learn
If you did not allow them
To get a little burn
Think of how much stronger
How much better they become
So think of me and remember
For you, I sacrificed my only Son.

ABOUT THE AUTHOR

Dawn E Johnecheck

Born in the little town of Charlevoix in northern Michigan, in late August of 1965, summers were always the favored time of year. Going swimming and spending days riding her bike around town or going for long walks are some Dawn's fondest memories.

Dawn met her husband in her early teens, but it wasn't till a number of years later that they started dating and got married. Since they've been together they moved all over the country and have lived in Tennessee, Arizona, Oregon and of course Michigan.

Dawn and her husband have three amazing children, who are grown and living their own lives. They keep in contact through phone calls, texts and social media. They are very proud of all three of them.

Dawn has written many unpublished poems and a couple of very short stories over the years, however until a few years ago never considered actually writing an entire book. It has been, at times exasperating and definitely a learning experience for her. She has felt truly lead throughout this entire process and thankful that God has gotten her through and guided her every step of the way.

Thank you, to all who read this book. Dawn's prayer is that it blesses you as much as writing it has blessed her.

If you have enjoyed this book you can go to her author page and/or her Facebook page and leave a review and comment. She loves to hear from readers and how this has affected them. Thank you and may God bless you greatly.

amazon.com/author/dawnj

www.facebook.com/dontsavethemanna

Made in the USA
Lexington, KY
05 April 2017